GROWING STRONG IN ~~THE~~ SEASONS OF LIFE:

SUMMER

GROWING STRONG IN
STRONG IN
THE
SEASONS
OF LIFE:
SUMMER

CHARLES R. SWINDOLL

FOREWORD BY
BILLY GRAHAM

WALKER AND COMPANY · NEW YORK

Large Print Edition by arrangement with Multnomah Press

First Large Print Edition published in the United States of America in 1989
    by Walker Publishing Company, Inc.

Published simultaneously in Canada by Thomas Allen & Son Canada, Limited, Markham, Ontario

Library of Congress Cataloging-in-Publication Data
Swindoll, Charles R.
    Growing strong in the seasons of life. Summer / Charles R.
Swindoll ; foreword by Billy Graham.—1st large print ed.
        p. cm.
    Originally published in 1 vol.: Growing strong in the seasons of
life. Portland, Or. : Multnomah Press, c1983.
    Bibliography: p.
    ISBN 0-8027-2636-4 (lg. print)
    1. Devotional exercises.   2. Summer—Religious aspects—
Christianity.   3. Large type books.   I. Title.   II. Title: Summer.
[BV4832.2.S8854   1989]
242'.2—dc20   89-34704
                                                                    CIP

Printed in the United States of America
10 8 6 4 2 1 3 5 7 9

Scripture quotations, unless otherwise marked, are taken from the New American Standard Bible. © The Lockman Foundation 1960, 1962, 1963, 1971, 1972, 1973, 1975, 1977, and are used by permission.

Verses marked TLB are taken from The Living Bible, © 1971 by Tyndale House Publishers, Wheaton, Ill. Used by permission.

Verses marked MLB were taken from The Modern Language Bible: The New Berkeley Version in Modern English, © 1945 by Gerit Verkuyl, and © 1959, 1969 by Zondervan Bible Publishers, and are used by permission.

Verses marked Phillips are taken from J. B. Phillips: The New Testament in Modern English, Revised Edition © J. B. Phillips 1958, 1960, 1972, and used by permission of Macmillan Publishing Co., Inc., New York; and Collins Publishers, London.

Verses marked NIV are taken from the Holy Bible: New International Version, © 1978 by the New York International Bible Society. Used by permission of Zondervan Bible Publishers.

With gratitude and delight I dedicate this volume to
EDGAR AND CANDEE NEUENSCHWANDER
who have been loving and supportive during the
cold winters, the changing springs, the hot
summers and the busy autumns of the
past twelve years of my life.
Through it all they have proven themselves faithful
friends both in season and out of season.

CONTENTS

CONTENTS

August

FOREWORD

On various occasions popular musical artists will release special albums that represent their best efforts. The titles are familiar to all of us: "The Best of Sinatra" . . . "The Best of Streisand" . . . "The best of Neil Diamond." It is not uncommon for these albums to push their way quickly to the top of the hit parade as music lovers listen again and again to their favorite artists doing the best work.

This volume by your friend and mine could be called "The Best of Charles Swindoll." For almost ten years this man has ministered to our world through books, several of which have become (and still are) best-sellers. All of us have come to expect high quality and unusual insights as we pick up another book to which he has put his pen . . . and we have not once been disappointed.

Here is another winner. *Growing Strong in the Seasons of Life* is not only a beautiful statement about four distinct "seasons," it is also a healthy and balanced diet of hope for the discouraged, a refuge for the hurting, a challenge for the weary, and a friend for the lonely. You will smile with understanding and you may even weep with compassion. You will appreciate how carefully Scripture is woven into the fabric of each page, sometimes boldly, but more often softly, artistically.

May you find the living Lord opening His arms of love to you as you move through each of these four seasons. Take your time. Walk slowly. Feel God's presence as you consider the days and weeks and years that He has given to you. Ask Him to bring new strength to your soul.

With delight I recommend "The Best of Charles Swindoll" to you. Here is a combination of words, phrases, and ideas you'll want to read again and again. A book for all seasons.

Billy Graham

INTRODUCTION

I am glad God changes the times and the seasons, aren't you?

Just think how dull things would become if He didn't paint nature's scenes in different colors several times a year. With inifinite creativity and remarkable regularity, He splashes white over brown and orange over grecn, giving such attcntion to dctail that we are often stunned with amazement.

Each of the four seasons offers fresh and vital insights for those who take the time to look and to think. Hidden beneath the surface are colorful yet silent truths that touch most every area across the landscape of our lives. As each three-month segment of every year holds its own mysteries and plays its own melodies, offering sights and smells, feelings and fantasies altogether distinct, so it is in the seasons of life. The Master is neither mute nor careless as He alters our times and changes our seasons. How wrong to trudge blindly and routinely through a lifetime of changing seasons without discovering answers to the new mysteries and learning to sing the new melodies! Seasons are designed to deepen us, to instruct us in the wisdom and ways of our God. To help us grow strong . . . like a tree planted by the rivers of water.

This is a book about one of the seasons: summer. It offers a series of suggestions and ideas to help you read

God's signals with a sensitive heart. Quietly and deliberately, we'll walk together through each scene, pondering the subtle shading as well as the obvious broad brush strokes from the Artist's hand. Let's take our time and leave room for our feelings to emerge. Let's sing in harmony with the Composer's music. Let's drink in the beauty of His handiwork. It will take time, so let's not hurry.

Our hope is to grow stronger and taller as our roots dig deeper in the soft soil along the banks of the river of life. And let's not fear the winds of adversity! The gnarled old twisted trees, beaten and buffeted by wind and weather along the ocean shores, tell their own stories of consistent courage. May God make us strong as the winds whip against us, my friend. Roots grow deep when the winds are strong. Let's commit ourselves to growing strong in the seasons of life.

Just before we embark on our journey, allow me a final few paragraphs concerning the composition of these thoughts.

When my family and I moved to Fullerton in the summer of 1971, I immediately began writing a weekly column in our church newsletter, which I called "Think It Over." I have continued that discipline to this day. Little did I realize the far-reaching effect these provocative articles would some day have on our generation! I must express my gratitude to the staff of Multnomah Press for their creative sensitivity and bold vision to publish this material in various formats and titles since 1977. *For Those Who Hurt; Starting Over; Standing Out; Killing Giants; Pulling Thorns; Make Up Your*

Mind; and *Encourage Me* have emerged from the original "Think It Over" articles. We have all been amazed to see how broadly God has used and continues to use each one of those books in peoples' lives. I confess, *I have been the most surprised of all!* (I've been tempted to publish the letters from those who wrote me, describing how God used the books in their lives.) This volume is a compilation of several previously published articles that first appeared in those books, plus numerous other columns never before published. I am especially indebted to Julie Cave and Larry Libby for their loving friendship over the years. Because of their skilled insight and creative editorial assistance, I was able to see how such varied columns fit so beautifully into the theme of the seasons.

And once again, I declare my gratitude to Helen Peters, my personal secretary, for her unselfish patience with me, along with her relentless devotion to the task of typing and retyping the original manuscript.

Now . . . let's walk together as God escorts us through the seasons. Let's listen closely to His voice as we observe the changing scenery. It might be wise for us to brace ourselves against those strong gusts of wind that inevitably accompany each season. But even the storms hear a message of encouragement for us:

Deeper roots make for stronger lives.

Charles R. Swindoll

GROWING STRONG IN

THE

SEASONS OF LIFE:

SUMMER

I can almost hear her singing it, can't you? Straight out of *Porgy and Bess* . . . the black lady rolls those big eyes and belts out:
"Summertime and the living' is easy, Fish are jumpin' and the cotton is high."

Makes us wanna git right down and run around the house barefoot, singing' the ole tune. We're talkin' cut-offs and tank tops, kite flyin', fun truckin', shaggin' flies, and *no school*. I mean, there ain't nothin' like those lazy, hazy days of summer, right? Makes no difference where we live, summer is easy living'! From the windswept hills of Tennessee to the craggy shoreline of Oregon . . . from the surfers off Santa Barbara to the racers in Indianapolis . . . from the rugged Baja Peninsula to nostalgic Cape Cod . . . from muggy Houston to soggy Seattle, when it's summertime, it's vacation time. A long-awaited season of relaxation and rest.

Speaking of rest, been doing much of it lately? Or is that resistance I'm feeling from you? If so, you're probably singing another song (it's usually in a minor key) with a hard-driving beat, a heavy rhythm, and lots of volume . . . sufficient to drown out all those comments from your family and a few close friends (and maybe your doctor?) urging you to add a little leisure to your life. Sure is easy to keep putting that off, isn't it? After all, there's a job to be done! *And* your to-do list isn't nearly accomplished. *And* you haven't reached your quota this month. *And* there are lots of folks depending on you. *And* if you plan to get ahead in this world, it's going to require a two-ended candle and a ton of energy. And . . . and . . . yes, I know, I know.

You want to know *how* I know? I hear those same messages inside my head. Being a high-achiever, work-ethic type myself, I've been beating that drum for almost half a century. ''Be responsible!'' ''Press on!'' ''Make things happen!'' ''Work hard!!'' ''Do it now!'' If anybody understands, I do.

But I can no longer ignore the necessity of the summer season in my life . . . nor can you, friend. If God considered this planet needed several months of summer, it stands to reason that His people are equally in need of refreshment and rest. He even says so:

> There remains therefore a Sabbath rest for the people of God. For the one who has entered His rest has himself also rested from his works, as God did from His. Let us therefore be diligent to enter that rest . . .
> Hebrews 4:9-11a).

Interesting (and convincing) command, isn't it? We are to be diligent to enter into rest. That doesn't mean a lazy, irresponsible life-style full of indolence and free of industry. No, this is first and foremost a *mental* rest, a quiet confidence in the living Lord. A refusal to churn, to fret, to strive.

Perhaps the following ''summer thoughts'' will help you live a little easier and, who knows, you may even become easier to with *with*!

2

Building Memories

"You guys go on without me. You'll have a great time—I'm sure of that. Sorry, family, but I have to work."

The place? Montgomery, Alabama.

The time? Several years ago.

The situation? A dad, who really loved his family and wanted them to enjoy a summer vacation, had to work. The press of business kept him tied to the office. But being committed to their happiness, he assured them of his desire that they take the trip and enjoy the fleeting summer days.

He helped them plan every day of the camping trip. They would load up the family station wagon, drive to California, camp up and down the coast, then travel back home together. Each day was carefully arranged—even the highways they would travel and the places they would stop. Dad knew their whole route, the time they would reach each state—planned almost to the hour—even when they would cross the Great Divide.

It's what he didn't tell them that made the difference.

The father took off work (he'd planned it all along) and arranged to have himself flown to an airport near where his family would be on that particular day of the trip. He had also arranged to have someone pick him up and drive him to a place where every car on that route had to pass. With a wide grin, he sat on his sleeping bag and waited for the arrival of that familiar station wagon packed full of kids and camping gear. When he spotted the station wagon, he stood up, stepped out onto the shoulder of the road, and stuck out his thumb.

Can you visualize it?

"Look! That guy looks just like . . . DAD!"

The family assumed he was a thousand miles away, sweating over a stack of papers. It's amazing they didn't drive off into a ditch or collapse from heart failure. Can you imagine the fun they had the rest of the way? And the memories they stored away in their mental scrapbook—could they ever be forgotten?

When later asked why he would go to all that trouble, the creative father replied, "Well . . . someday I'm going to be dead. When that happens, I want my kids and wife to say, "You know, Dad was a lot of fun.""[1]

Talk about a unique domestic game plan! What an outstanding model of a father who wants to be remembered for more than just the basics . . .

"*. . . turn out the lights.*"
"*Did you get the bed made?*"
"*Get out there and cut the grass.*"
"*No, we can't. I gotta work.*"
"*How much does it cost?*"
"*That's too much trouble, dear. Let's be practical.*"
"*Hold it down—I can't hear the news.*"

Oh—but there's so much more in life! The beautiful music of living is composed, practiced, and perfected in the harmony of home. The freedom to laugh long and loudly . . . the encouragement to participate in creative activities . . . the spontaneity of relaxed relationships that plant memories and deepen our roots in the rich, rare soil of authentic happiness. Couldn't this be included in the "all things" Paul mentioned in Romans 8:32 and 1 Timothy 6:17? The apostle tells us that our God *"richly supplies us with all things to enjoy."*

We're missing it—God's best—if the fun memories are being eclipsed by the fierce ones. The world outside the family circle is dark enough. When the light goes out *within* the circle . . . how great is the darkness.

If life with mom and dad has become more of an endurance course than a refreshing catalyst, then your prime time project isn't too tough to identify. Too many of us are beginning to resemble stern-faced East German guards patrolling the wall rather than approachable, believable parents, building happy memories. And maybe even a few crazy ones, too. Don't worry, God can handle it. He's got a great sense of humor. He made *you,* didn't He?

I'd much rather my brood remember me as the dad who tossed their mother fully clothed into the swimming pool—and lived to tell the story—than the preacher who frowned too much, yelled too loud, talked too long . . . and died too young.

Deepening Your Roots
1 Timothy 6:17; Luke 15:22-32; Psalm 145:3-7

Branching Out
1. Do something creative and special today with your family, a friend, or a coworker, that is totally unexpected and will always bring back a fond, wonderful memory.
2. Bring your camera out of hiding and take some candid shots of someone you like. Get the film developed and create a mini-scrapbook for him.

Living it Up

Pussy cat, pussy cat, where have you been?
I've been to London to look at the queen.
Pussy cat, pussy cat, what did you there?
I frightened a little mouse under her chair.

Stupid cat. She had the chance of a lifetime. All of London stretched out before her. Westminster Abbey. The British Museum. Ten Downing Street. Trafalgar Square. The House of Parliament. The Marble Arch in Hyde Park. She could've heard the London Philharmonic or scrambled up an old wooden lamp post to watch the changing of the guard. I doubt that she even cared she was within walking distance of St. Paul's Cathedral. She probably didn't even realize it was the historic Thames rushing by beneath that big rusty bridge she scampered across chasing more mice.

After all, she didn't even scope out the queen as Her Majesty stood before her. Not this cat. She is such a mouseaholic, she can't stop the same old grind even when she's in London. What a bore!

Can you imagine the scene as her husband meet her at the plane at LA International?

"Hi, Fluff. How was it? What did ya' see? Tell me all about it."

7

"Well, Tom, it all started when I saw this little mouse under the queen's throne. From then on it was just like here. I chased mice all over London. Do you realize how many mice there are in that city?"

"You what? You mean to tell me you spent ten days in London and all you can say for it is this stuff about mice!"

There is an old Greek motto that says:

YOU WILL BREAK THE BOW
IF YOU KEEP IT ALWAYS BENT.

Which, being translated loosely from the original, means, "There's more to being a cat than tracking mice." Or, "There's more to life than hard work." Loosening the strings on our bow means when we have some leisure, we live it up. We deliberately erase from our minds that we are a cop or an engineer or a lawyer or a preacher or a salesman or a prof. We back off the strings and blow it. We break the up-tight mold and do stuff that helps us stay sane. And fun to be with. And whole people. We consciously decide against playing everything safe . . . at least for a little while . . . as we gain some perspective that our rut normally keeps us from seeing.

Which means if we spend a week in Hawaii, we don't pinch pennies. We don't even talk about it. Or think about it. The same applies to an evening at a classy restaurant or a night at the Hollywood Bowl or a weekend at Aspen.

Or if we take a cruise, we don't focus on dieting. We refuse to be like the woman on the Titanic who, as she climbed into the lifeboat, facing an uncertain future, sobbed in anguish, "If I had known this was going to happen, I'd have had the chocolate mousse for dessert!"

Or if we go to the slopes, we don't chop firewood or change our oil or worry about the papers stacking up in our driveway. We get out there in all that snow and have fun! And when we are too doggone tired to take one more ride on the lift, we crawl back on the shuttle, slump down in the seat and laugh out loud.

Or if we shoot the rapids, we attack those babies! *Full bore!* We scream and spit and gag on a raft full of water as we forget all about being responsible, sensible, professional, and proper. The aches and pains, we'll worry about later. Right now it's "let 'er rip!" That applies to an afternoon at Dodger Stadium or an evening with the Rams.

Maybe that's what Jim Eliot meant when he wrote, "Wherever you are, be all there. Live to the hilt every situation you believe to be the will of God. "That's another way of putting the familiar line out of Paul's letter:

> And whatever you do in word or deed, do all in the name of the Lord Jesus, giving thanks through Him to God the Father (Colossians 3:17).

Ever followed that to its logical conclusion? Unless I miss the point entirely, it takes the galling guilt out of living it up. It means we are free to enjoy to full measure our leisure. Even if it is *really* expensive. Even if it is wild 'n' wooly. Even if it is fattening or crazy or *completely* out of character.

But one word of advice . . . better keep it to yourself. A lot of folks never go anywhere without a thermometer, a raincoat, a full tank of gas, a gargle, a hot-water bottle, aspirin, a change of socks, plenty of hair spray, and a parachute. Oh, yeah, they're also the ones who keep asking, "What time is it?" And, "How much does this cost?" And, "Are you sure everybody will understand?"

They're the same ones who would commend Fluff for "behaving herself" in London.

Deepening Your Roots
Deuteronomy 6: 1,2; 1 Chronicles 15:25-29; 1 Chronicles
    29:6-28

Branching Out
1. Do something that is totally out of character for you, and causes others to laugh.
2. Blow it today! Be extravagant; don't pinch pennies. And don't you dare feel guilty about it afterwards.
3. Block out some leisure time on your calendar to ensure you'll take some days off for refreshment.

Man's Quest

Greece said . . . Be wise, know yourself.
Rome said . . . Be strong, discipline yourself.
Judaism says . . . Be holy, conform yourself.
Epicureanism says . . . Be sensuous, enjoy yourself.
Education says . . . Be resourceful, expand yourself.
Psychology says . . . Be confident, fulfill yourself.
Materialism says . . . Be acquisitive, please yourself.
Pride says . . . Be superior, promote yourself.
Ascetism says . . . Be inferior, suppress yourself.
Diplomacy says . . . Be reasonable, control yourself.
Communism says . . . Be collective, secure yourself.
Humanism says . . . Be capable, trust yourself.
Philanthropy says . . . Be unselfish, give yourself.

And on and on and on goes the quest of man. No wonder people are confused! Pick any thought-dish from this smorgasbord of human philosophy, then digest it completely . . . and you will find yourself suffering from the worst case of indigestion imaginable. It may smell good and even satisfy your rhetorical palate during the time you are consuming it . . . but it will leave you hungry, uneasy, and searching for something else to satisfy.

Rollo May's words often interrupt my thinking as I ponder the plight of searching men and women today:

> It is an old and ironic habit of human beings to run faster when we have lost our way.

And so it is! Look across your office desk tomorrow and chances are you'll be observing a living example of someone still searching, still running to find inner satisfaction. Step out in front of your apartment or home tomorrow morning and look both ways . . . listen to the roar of automobiles . . . study the dwellings surrounding you. Those sights and sounds represent people who have, like Little Bo-Peep's sheep, "lost their way," and, tragedy upon tragedy—they don't know where to find it. Many of them have tried hard to "be religious" or "live by the golden rule" or "tie a knot and hang on" or "be sincere," but they're still running blind and bored and baffled.

They are attempting to fill the inner vacuum with *everything but the only thing*. You name it, it's being tried. As Henry Thoreau declared:

> The mass of men lead lives of quiet desperation

Robert Ingersol, the bold and brilliant agnostic, spent many years of his life opposing and attacking the Scriptures and Christ's claims. On his deathbed . . . at the end of his race, he uttered:

> Life is a narrow veil between the cold and barren peaks of two eternities. We strive in vain to look beyond the heights. We cry aloud, and the only answer is the echo of our wailing cry.

12

Ingersol's pursuit is best described in the bumper sticker I saw on my way to work:

DON'T FOLLOW ME . . . I'M LOST

Pontius Pilate, Judea's notorious governor, stood eyeball to eyeball with Jesus of Nazareth. In the judicial process of interrogation, he heard Christ refer to "everyone who is of the truth," to which Pilate replied, "What is truth?" That question hangs heavily on the thin wire of reason in many a mind this very hour. Pilate never waited for an answer. He whirled away in confused disgust. He should have stopped running and waited for the answer. Jesus could have told him that He alone had satisfying words of life . . . for He alone *is* "the way, the truth, and the life" (John 14: 6).

Christianity is not a system of human philosophy nor a religious ritual nor a code of moral ethics—it is the impartation of divine life through Christ. Apart from the Way there is no going . . . apart from the Truth there is no knowing . . . apart from the Life there is no living.

God says . . . Be in Christ, rest yourself.

Deepening Your Roots

1 John 3:16-20; Matthew 11:25-30; Psalm 62:5-8; Psalm 91:1,2

Branching Out

1. Look at the pace of your life today. In a hurry? Rushing? Force yourself to take thirty minutes to relax; calm down and slowly do a task.
2. Decide from the list of philosophies which one you lean towards. Spot an area in your life where this philosophy is evident and replace it with God's perspective.
3. Discard an object in your house that is not in keeping with God's philosophy, or contends for time which might otherwise be spent in enjoying moments with God.

Fathers

In an age of equal rights and equal time, it's only fair to give the dads equal attention. Over a month ago the moms were standing in the spotlight. Move over, ladies . . . make way for the men, in fact, a very select group of men—*fathers*. It's timely to do that since summer is the season for Fathers Day.

As if you didn't know! Every store window, newspaper, and national magazine in America has been parading gift ideas before your eyes for the past thirty days. Families have been wondering whether to wrap us in robes, fill us with food, surprise us with skis, tickle us with tools, or just cover us with kisses. If I know dads, most of 'em are going to blush no matter what you do. They are so used to providing, receiving is kinda weird. Occasionally, it's downright embarrassing! Most dads are quick to say to their families (with pardonable pride):

Look—sit back and relax . . . and leave the striving to us!

Think about your father, okay? Meditate on what that one individual has contributed to you. Think about his influence over you, his investment in you, his insights to you. Study his face . . . the lines that are now in-

15

delibly etched on your mind. Listen again to the echo of his voice . . . that infectious laugh . . . those unique expressions that emerge through the miracle of memory. Feel his hand around yours . . . his strong, secure arm across your shoulders. That grip that once communicated a strange mixture of gentleness and determination . . . compassion and masculinity . . . "I understand" and "Now, straighten up!" Watch his walk. No other walk like his, is there? Those sure steps. That inimitable stridce. Arms swinging and back arched just so.

Best of all, remember his exemplary character. The word is *integrity*. As you read this, pause and recall just one or two choice moments in your past when he stood alone . . . when he stood by you . . . in a time of storm. When he protected you from the bitter blast of life's harsh consequences. When he said, "Honey, I forgive you," instead of, "You ought to be ashamed!"

In the wake of such a legacy which time can never rob, give God thanks. That's all. Just thanks the Giver of every good and perfect gift for the meaningful marks your dad has branded on the core of your character . . . the wholesome habits he has woven into the fabric of your flesh. While meandering through this forest of nostalgia, stop at the greak oak named Proverbs and reflect upon the words the wise man carved into its bark twenty-nine centuries ago:

A righteous man walks in his integrity—
How blessed are his sons [and daughters] *after him.*

Ah, how true!

Our Lord declares that you are the beneficiary in a perpetual, paternal policy. For the balance of your life, you receive the dividends from your father's wise and sacrificial investments in "integrity stock." Most of those dividends were unknown and unclaimed until you were grown. How many of us now find ourselves richly endowed!

He is not perfect. He would be the first to admit it. Nor is he infallible, much to his own dismay. Nor altogether fair . . . nor always right. But there's one thing he is—always and altogether—*he is your dad* . . . the only one you'll ever have. And quite frankly, there's only one thing he needs on Father's Day—plain and simple—he needs to hear you say four words:

Dad, I love you.

That's the best gift you can give. If you give him your love, you can keep all the other stuff. Come to think of it, it's the most important gift of all.

Deepening Your Roots
Exodus 20:12; Ephesians 6:1-4; Hebrews 12:7-11; 1 Kings
    2:1-4;
1 Kings 3:3-15

Branching Out
1. Write your dad a loving note and remind him of a special
   memory he has given you that shares how deep his love
   is for you.
2. Write down ten things about your dad that you can thank
   God for. Go ahead . . . thank God!
3. Rather than buying your dad a gift, make him something
   or do something special for him that he's always talked
   about doing, but never had time for. Build a memory
   together.

Anniversaries

I don't need to tell *you* what I think of marriage and the family. You who know me already know. If I'm ever guilty of grinding an axe, I suppose it would be the home . . . that place where life makes up its mind. No need to add to what you've heard from me over and over again—*or is there?* Maybe so.

There is a reason I am prompted to say more. I celebrated my twenty-fifth wedding anniversary not too long ago. Seems incredible. I remember in my younger years looking upon those who celebrated their quarter-of-a-century anniversary as folks one hop away from a wheelchair. amazing how times flies! About the time your face clears up, your mind gets fuzzy. Or at least a little *misty*. Why? I can think of four reasons.

MEMORIES. Those ''watercolor memories,'' as Streisand sings it, have a way of washing across one's mind, like the surf upon the shore, when anniversaries come. Funny memories. Also painful ones. Yet all of them dripping with nostalgia. Like our honeymoon—a colossal comedy of errors. And our eighteen months of forced separation when we were 8000 miles apart, thanks to the military. My midstream switch in careers . . . back to school, that tiny apartment, those disciplined, mind-stretching hours poring over the books. The births of our four (plus the loss of two we never got to see) and those energy-draining years from diapers to kindgergarten. Wow! How much we learned together . . . how deeply our roots grew together . . . how rugged and long were some of those roads we traveled together.

An anniversary says, "Don't ever forget the memories. They are imperishable."

CHANGES. You just don't live two-and-a-half decades with the same person without doing a flip-flop in several major areas of your life. I suppose the single most significant one with me is in the realm of sensitivity. I have learned to read between the lines, to hear feelings that are never spoken, to see anguish or anger, joy or jealousy, confusion or compassion in faces that communicate what the tongue may not declare. And what an authority I was twenty-five years ago! I had it all wired—but what a difference a wife and a pack of kids make! God has used them to temper my intensity. The change from an opinionated dogmatist to more of an openminded learner was really needed. And really overdue. That process, by the way, is still going on.

An anniversary says, "Be thankful for the changes. They are important."

DEPENDENCE. My marriage has taught me that I am neither all-sufficient nor totally self-sufficient. I *need* a wife. I need her support, her insight, her discernment, her counsel, her love, her presence, and her efficiency. She is not my crutch . . . but she is my God-given companion and partner, ever aware of my moods and my needs. She hears my secrets and keeps them well. She knows my faults and forgives them often. She feels my failures and apprehensions and encourages me through them. For ten full years Cynthia was unaware of the fact that I needed her. I was one of those husbands who plowed through life like a freight train—bullish, intimidating, selfish, and on top. Finally, the cracks began to show. Couldn't hide 'em any longer. Of saying things like, "I'm wrong . . . I'm really sorry." And even coming up front with my wife and delcaring how very much I depend on her to help me hang in there.

An anniversary says, "You don't have to make it on your own. Your partner is irreplaceable."

DREAMS. One final thing is worth mentioning. Dreams are what you anticipate as a couple, then watch God pull off. Sometimes they are little things, like working in the garden together, dropping a few seeds and seeing the sprouts, then the fruit. Or praying together about one of the children . . . you know, asking God to grab his heart and soften his spirit. As that dream happens, you smile at each other. You understand. Occasionally, the dream is a big thing . . . calling for sustained sacrifice, mutually shared. Like getting through school. Or remodeling your home. Or getting out of debt. When the reality finally occurs, no words can describe the pleasure of the long embrace, that kiss of profound accomplishment.

An anniversary says, "Think of the dreams you have weathered together. They are intimate accomplishments."

Our silver anniversary is a beautiful combination of

memories, changes, growing dependence, and dreams. They date back to June 18, 1955, when a couple of kids said, "I do" and committed themselves to each other for life . . . having no idea what threatening storms lay ahead of us or what unspeakable joys would weld us together. For life.

I am a grateful husband. May God be praised for the genius of marriage and the thrill of celebrating it annually with the one I love.

Deepening Your Roots
Book of Ruth; Hebrews 13:1-6

Branching Out
1. Name one way you've changed in the past twenty-five years. Ask someone the same question.
2. What is a memory for which you are thankful? Tell someone about it and why you're thankful.
3. Whether it's your anniversary or not, celebrate your marriage or a friendship by doing something special this evening. You don't have to be elaborate—but do something—even if it's popping popcorn together!

Overexpecting

When you stop achieving long enough to think about it, our world is full of overexpecters. They are in every profession, most of the schools, many of the shops, and (dare I say it?) all the churches.

To the overexpecter, enough is never enough. There's always room for improvement, always an area or two that isn't quite up to snuff, always something to criticize. Always. The overexpecter uses words like "ought" and "should" and loves sentences that include "must" and "more." To them, "work harder" and "reach higher" are the rule rather than the exception. When you're around them you get the distinct impression that no matter how hard you've tried, you haven't measured up. And what's worse, *you never will*. Overexpecters don't say that, but the meaning oozes out of their frowns and glares. Sooner or later your motivation is sapped as demands and expectations replace excitement with guilt. The killer is that final moment when you realize you have become a weary slave of the impossible.

Fun fades. Laughter leaves. And what remains? This won't surprise anybody: The tyranny of the urgent. The uptight, the essential, the expected—*always* the expected. Which, being interpreted, means, "the making of a coronary."

It's like my friend Tim Hansel's 1973 journal entry:

When laughter fades
the tendency toward self-absorption
squeezes the light to a pinpoint.
Morning only intimidates you into another day
and creativity no longer has the energy to care.

Because nobody screws up enough courage to tell overexpecters where to get off, these things keep happening:

The little child loses his love for art because he is told time and gain to stop coloring outside the lines. Parents are often overexpecters.

The wife erodes in her joy around the house because she never seems to please the man she married. Husbands are often overexpecters.

- The gifted and competent employee gets an ulcer because the boss finds it next to impossible to say two monosyllabic words, "good job." Employers are often overexpecters.

- The once-dedicated, motivated pastor in a small church finally decides to change careers because he realizes he will never please his people. Church members are often overexpecters.

The high school athlete chooses to hang it up at midseason because he knows that no matter what, he'll never satisfy. Coaches are often overexpecters.

And, yes congregations get tired of being beaten and bruised with jabs, hooks, and uppercuts from pulpits. Preachers are often overexpecters.

So what's the answer? Obviously it's not the opposite

extreme. Few people who are healthy enjoy mediocrity. Life without challenge is about as exciting as watching shadows change on a sundial. No. I haven't got all the answers, but when I think over my own tendency toward overexpecting, six words help a lot. Honesty. Reality. Acceptance. Tolerance. Acknowledgement. Encouragement.

I frequently think of Jesus as the Model. He promised people "rest" if they would come to Him, not an endless list of unrealistic expectations. He even said His yoke would be "easy" and His burden "light." *He was something else*. Still is!

All of us high-achievers need big doses of the counsel that must have emerged out of a homespun cocoon on some screened-in back porch south of the Mason-Dixon Line many years ago:

> When I works, I works hard;
> When I sits, I sits loose;
> When I thinks, I fall asleep.

Deepening Your Roots
Proverbs 11:7; Haggai 1:1-12; Luke 6:32-36; John 5-4-43

Branching Out
1. Name an area in which you expect too much of yourself. Now, allow yourself a more realistic expectation:
2. What's something others expect from you that is a "fair" expectation which you should meet, but usually don't? Work this week on fulfilling that expectation.

In the Shade of a Juniper

A major portion of our eye troubles could probably be diagnosed "ingrownius eyeballitus." Ingrown eyeballs. It strikes us all. In both dramatic and subtle ways, the stubborn enemy of our souls urges us to look ever inward instead of outward and upward. He whispers little nothings in our ears. He reminds us of how unappreciated and ill-treated we are . . . how important yet overlooked . . . how gifted yet ignored . . . how capable yet unrecognized . . . how bright yet eclipsed.

This clever adversary slips into the office of the faithful worker who has been bypassed, unpromoted. Looking up from his cluttered desk, the worker's mind is suddenly swamped with the silt of self-pity. Slipping down the hall and into the sickroom of the sufferer, the enemy pauses long enough to announce: "You've been forgotten. No one cares about you—not really. Out of sight, out of mind." Kneeling behind the bench warmer he whispers, "Face it, man, first string is out of reach. You'll never make it." To the unemployed he says, "No chance!" To the divorced he says, "No place!" To the bereaved he says, "No hope!" To the struggling he says, "No way!"

The most damaging impact of self-pity is its ultimate

end. Cuddle and nurse it as an infant and you'll have on your hands in a brief period of bitterness and paranoia throughout your system. A frown will soon replace your smile. A pungent criticism will replace a pleasant, ''I understand.'' Suspicion and resentment will submerge your selfish island like a tidal wave. You will soon discover that the sea of self-pity has brought with it prickly urchins of doubt, despair, and even the desire to die.

An exaggeration? A wild imagination? If you think so, sit with me beneath the shade of a juniper tree located at 19 First Kings, the address of a prophet named Elijah. The leather-girded prophet had just finished mopping up a victory over Ahab and his Baal-worshiping cronies. God stamped His approval upon Elijah in such a way that all Israel realized he was God's mouthpiece. At this point Jezebel, Ahab's spouse (he was her mouse), declared and predicted Elijah's death within twenty-four hours. Surely the seasoned prophet had faced criticism before. He lived with bad press and constant threats—all prophets do. That's par for the course! But this threat somehow found its mark in the chink of his armor.

Elijah ran for his life. Finally, ninety miles later, he collapsed beneath a juniper tree. Overwhelmed with self-pity, the prophet whined, ''I've had enough . . . take away my life. I've got to die sometime, and it might as well be now.''

Later on he admitted:

I have worked very hard for the Lord God of the heavens; but the people of Israel have broken their covenant with you and torn down your altars and killed your prophets,

27

and only I am left; and now they are trying to kill me, too (1 Kings 19:10, TLB).

There you have it. Self-pity in the raw. Elijah's eyes were so ingrown he saw two of everything—except God. He felt unloved, cast off, and out of it. Most of all, he believed his situation so isolated him that he only was left. Nobody else was near, and in the prophet's mind, that included God. Self-pity is the smog that pollutes and obscures the light of the Son. The more you're out in it, the deeper it hurts. The more your eyes shed tears, the greater the sting of loneliness.

But God didn't rebuke His man. He didn't club him nor did He strike him dead. Instead, He encouraged him to take a long rest and enjoy a catered meal or two. Jehovah helped Elijah get his eyes off himself and his situation. Gently, He prodded the prophet to focus anew on his God. A little later, the Lord gave him a close friend named Elisah with whom he might share his life and his load.

Feeling sorry for yourself today? Caught in that ancient "sin-drome" of self-pity? Why not try God's remedy: A good, well-deserved mental rest where you stop trying to work things out *yourself* . . . a decent, well-balanced diet . . . a long, well-needed look at your Savior in His word . . . topped off with some quality time with a friend.

You will be amazed at the outcome. You may even discover that what you thought was approaching blindness was only an advanced case of ingrown eyeballs.

Deepening Your Roots
Proverbs 4:20-27; Luke 11:33-36; John 9:1-41; 2 Corinthians
   4:16-18

[handwritten: man born blind]

[handwritten: Vision: physical & spiritual]

Branching Out
1. Eat well-balanced meals today (not junk food), plus take
   time to read and think and allow God to refresh your
   spirit.
2. Are you getting a case of "ingrown eyeballs"? Call a
   friend for some fresh perspective.

[handwritten notes:]

Prov.
Keep eyes open to walk safe path
+ avoid falling into evil.

Luke —
Eye is lamp of body.
Keep the light of true faith
burning — lest we be full
of darkness — & cannot
see the hazardous paths
ahead...

2 Cor. 4:16-18
Keep our eyes on eternal truths.

17-18-19
I Kings — Elijah.

Insight

Are you ready for a surprise? You blink twenty-five times every minute. Each blink takes you about one-fifth of a second. Therefore, if you take a ten-hour automobile trip, averaging forty miles per hour, you will drive twenty miles with your eyes *closed*.

I know a fact far more surprising than that. Some people go through *life* with their eyes closed. They look but don't really "see" . . . they observe the surface but omit the underneath . . . they focus on images but not issues . . . vision is present but perception is absent. If life were a painting, they would see colors but no genius in the strokes of the brush. If it were a journey, they would notice a road but no majestic, awesome scenery. If it were a meal, they would eat and drink but overlook the exquisite beauty of the china and the delicate touch of wine in the sauce. If it were a poem, they would read print on the page but miss altogether the passion of the poet. Remove insight and you suddenly reduce life to *existence* with frequent flashes of boredom and indifference.

Those without insight dwell mainly in the realm of the obvious . . . the expected . . . the essentials. The dimensions that interest them are length and width, not depth. Please understand, I do not mean to be critical of those who *cannot* go deeper . . . but of those who can but *will not*. I'm not pointing my finger at inability but rather refusal.

As a concrete illustration, take the boatload of disciples in Mark, chapter 6. Immediately after Jesus had miraculously fed thousands of people with a few loaves and fish, He sent His men away in a boat as He slipped off to a quiet place on the mountain to pray. A storm later broke upon the sea and they were filled with panic. He came to their rescue shortly thereafter and calmed the sea as He stilled the wind and assured them there was no reason to be afraid. Mark makes a comment worth remembering:

> . . . they were greatly astonished, for they had not gained any insight from the incident of the loaves, but their heart was hardened (vv. 51b-52).

It wasn't that they were unable to understand. They didn't want to understand! William Barclay of Glasgow says, "Their minds were obtuse." That was the root problem. Those men were insensitive, dull, blunt-brained. They weren't ding-a-lings by nature, but by choice—and therein rested not the tragedy but the blame! They didn't need Jesus' pity as much as they deserved a rebuke. By then they had been sufficiently exposed to their miracle-working Master to respond with keen insight to their circumstances. Had they applied what they observed earlier that day when the thousands were fed, their response to the storm would have been insightful.

Hebrews 5 is addressed to similar disciples today. Hours upon hours have been logged under the teaching of the Word, and opportunities to use those truths have been legion. But what does this passage say? It says some have become "dull of hearing"—thick, lazy, sluggish, lacking insight. Maturity—the result of mixing insight with practice—is rare today . . . and so the discernment between good and evil, brought on by "trained senses," is frequently conspicuous by its absence.

What are a few practical rewards? Parents with insight usually raise kids that are secure, fulfilled, relaxed, free to forge out ideas and to think. Single adults with insight won't feel they *must* marry—the sooner the better. Teachers with insight create an atmosphere conducive to learning. Bosses with insight develop employees and remain sensitive to surrounding needs. Students with insight learn far more than the required subject—they indeed glean an education.

I challenge you: Open your eyes! Think! Apply! Dig! Listen! There's a lot of difference between necessary blinking and unnecessary blindness.

Deepening Your Roots
Mark 6:45-56; Luke 24:36-45; Colossians 3:2; Hebrews 5:1-14; 1 Peter 1:13-15; 1 Kings 4:29

Branching Out
1. Next time you're forced to think, don't back off. Dig in. Interact. Think!
2. Rather than just read today's Scripture, study it. Ponder over each verse. Write down a new insight.

Appraising Life

It's been awhile since you took stock of where you're going, hasn't it? And how about an evaluation of the kids? Or your marriage? Or your own future? You know what I mean, trimming off the fat of lazy thinking and taking a lean, hard look at the years remaining.

As I write these words, I'm looking ahead to my forty-fourth birthday. If Christ doesn't return (and I don't die in the meantime), I figure I've got about twenty to twenty-five remaining years of effective service.

How old are you? How many years lie between now and when you turn sixty-five or seventy? It's high time you came to terms with your future, isn't it?

And if that doesn't grab you, consider your *family* in the next decade. In only ten years Cynthia and I will have a son twenty-seven years old, a daughter twenty-five, another daughter twenty-one, and our "baby" will be eighteen! It is possible that none of our four will be living at home . . . in only ten years. Seems impossible. Especially since our place today resembles a cross between Grand Central Station, the Indianapolis 500, and the San Diego Zoo. But it won't always be that way. As the old newsreel says, "Time marches on."

Occasions set aside for evaluation and regrouping are

needed. Even the sports world has its time out and sev-enth-inning stretch and pit stop and half time, so why shouldn't we? Force yourself to pull off the road, put your pace into neutral, and ask some hard questions. Here are a few worth personal consideration:

1. Am I really happy, genuinely challenged and ful-filled in life?
2. In light of eternity, am I making a consistent in-vestment for God's glory and His cause?
3. Is the direction my life is now taking leading me toward a satisfying and meaningful future?
4. Can I honestly say that I am in the nucleus of God's will for me?

And for the kids:

1. Am I spending sufficient time with the children so that they know I love and accept them and care very much about their future?
2. Am I communicating life goals, a proper value sys-tem, a standard of moral purity, a drive for excel-lence, and commitment to loyalty, integrity, generosity, and honesty to my children? Do they really *know* how I feel about these things?
3. Are they aware that they are worthwhile and val-uable? Are they growing up to be positive, confi-dent, secure, highly esteemed young men and women?
4. When they leave the nest, will they be able to stand alone?

Please read General Douglas MacArthur's prayer for his son. Read the words slowly, deliberately, and—if possible—aloud.

34

Build me a son, O Lord, who will be strong enough to know when he is weak, and brave enough to face himself when he is afraid; one who will be proud and unbending in honest defeat, and humble and gentle in victory.

Build me a son whose wishbone will not be where his backbone should be; a son who will know Thee and that to know himself is the foundation stone of knowledge.

Lead him, I pray, not in the path of ease and comfort, but under the stress and spur of difficulties and challenge. Here let him learn to stand up in the storm; here let him learn compassion for those who fail.

Build me a son whose heart will be clean, whose goal will be high; a son who will master himself before he seeks to master other men; one who will learn to laugh, yet never forget how to weep; one who will reach into the future, yet never forget the past.

And after all these things are his, add, I pray, enough of a sense of humor, so that he may always be serious, yet never take himself too seriously. Give him humility, so that he may always remember the simplicity of greatness, the open mind of true wisdom, the meekness of true strength.

Then I, his father, will dare to whisper, "I have not lived in vain."

For what are you asking the Lord on behalf of your life and your children? I challenge you, stop long enough to think it over. And don't just think, get alone and *write down* your thoughts, your dreams, your aspirations. Refuse to let tonight's television programs or some insignificant activity interrupt this necessary discipline. If you put if off, you may lose the urgency you sense right now.

*Home is a lot of things . . . but mainly
it is the place where life make up its mind.*

Solomon, the wise, offers solid counsel:

Remember also your Creator . . . before the evil days
come and the years draw near when you will say, "I have
no delight in them"; . . . Remember Him before . . . the
spirit will return to God who gave it (Ecclesiastes 12:1,
6-7).

By doing these things—and following through with
the necessary changes that will enable you to accomplish
your plans—you will get back on target. And best of
all, you will be able to say, "I have not lived in vain."

Deepening Your Roots
Ecclesiastes 12:1-14; Proverbs 30:7-9; 2 Corinthians 5:6-10;
 Philippians 3:4;
1 Peter 1:3-9

Branching Out
1. How many, and what people, do you think will be living
 with you in ten years?
2. Tonight answer the question: "What are you asking the
 Lord on behalf of your life?"
3. Determine two new life goals and write them down.

Acting Medium

The children worked long and hard on their own little cardboard shack. It was to be a special spot—a clubhouse—where they could meet in solemn assembly or just laugh, play games, and fool around. As they thought long and hard about their rules, they came up with three rather perceptive ones:

1. Nobody act big.
2. Nobody act small.
3. Everybody act medium.[2]

Not bad theology!

In different words, God says the very same thing:

> . . . give preference to one another in honor (Romans 12:10).
> . . . whoever wishes to become great among you shall be your servant, and whoever wishes to be first among you shall be your slave (Matthew 20:26-27).
> Let another praise you, and not your own mouth; a stranger, and not your own lips (Proverbs 27:2).

Just "act medium." Believable, honest, human, thoughtful, and down-to-earth. Regardless of your elevated position or high pile of honors or row of degrees or endless list of achievements, just stay real. Work hard

37

at counteracting the celebrity syndrome. Junk any idea that you deserve some kind of pat on the back or wristwatch for a job well done. Who did you do it for, anyway? If you did it for God, He has an infinite number of unseen ways to reward you. If you did it for man, no wonder you're clawing for glory!

But it's so subtle. So easy to draw out that praise for yourself, isn't it? Especially around the house when you do a few extras.

A certain firm has made headlines out of deflating overblown egos. Its well-trained employees accept contracts to squash juicy pies into the faces of pompous individuals. In its first few months, over sixty hits were made at $35 per splash! All on disbelieving, immaculately dressed, prim-and-proper victims.

Imagine this scene: A dignified, well-tailored executive vice-president waits for the elevator to open on the eighteenth floor. As he steps out, a stranger whips a pie out of a cardboard box and splosh! Giving the pie a professional twist, the hit-man jumps into the elevator headed for the main floor. There stands Vice President Shmotz . . . his once-spotless suit, matching vest, and tie now dripping with lemon meringue goo and crust.

An employee of the pie-tossing company said, "A pie in the face brings a man's dignity down to where it should be and puts the big guys on the same level with everyone else."[3]

Even Biola College weathered the recent pie-throwing rage. No one was safe from the meringue gang—neither the professors nor even the school's great-hearted president who took it on the chin like a champ. I'd hate to think how many college presidents would have responded with their superguarded, highly polished egos smeared with bright gold pumpkin pie and whipping cream. I wonder how many would "act medium."

Again what was it the Son of David said?

Let another praise you . . . and not your own lips.

Meaning what? Meaning no self-reference to some enviable accomplishment. Meaning no desire to manipulate and manufacture praise. Meaning authentic surprise when applauded. Genuine, rare humility—regardless.

One final warning. Don't try to fake it. False humility stinks worse than raw conceit. The answer is not in trying to *appear* worthless and "wormy" but in consistently taking notice of others' achievements, recognizing others' skill and contributions . . . and saying so. Got

Got the rules memorized? "Nobody act big. Nobody act small. Everybody act medium." Such good advice from a clubhouse full of kids, who, by the way, are pretty good at practicing what they preach.

And they also laugh out loud when you get a pie in the kisser. Believe me, I know.

Deepening Your Roots
1 Peter 5:5,6; Matthrew 20:20-28;

Branching Out
1. Try not to use the word "I" today. Everytime you hear it roll off your lips, chalk up 10¢. At the end of the day give the loot to your kids or to a friend.
2. Don't praise yourself or ask for commendation (i.e., How did I do?).

A Rare and Remarkable Virtue

Perhaps you've uttered the American's Prayer at some anxious moment recently:

Lord, give me patience . . . and I want it *right now!*

This rare and remarkable virtue is within the *and-so-forth* section in Galatians chapter 5. You know how we quote that passage . . . "the fruit of the Spirit is love, joy, peace, *and-so-forth*." That lazy habit has caused a very important series of virtues to become forgotten. Allow me to quote Galatians 5:22-23—in full.

But the fruit of the Spirit is love, joy, peace, patience, kindness, goodness, faithfulness, gentleness, self-control; against such things there is no law.

Notice, please, the fourth on the list. Patience. The original Greek term unloads a lot of meaning upon us. MAKROTHUMIA is the term, and it's a compound word. MAKROS means "long or far," and THUMOS means "hot, anger, or wrath." Putting it together, we come up with "long-anger.' You've heard the English expression "short-tempered"? Well, I suppose we could coin an expression for patience—*long-tempered*—and not miss the accurate meaning very far.

Generally speaking, the Greek word is not used of patience in regard to things or events, but of patience in regard to *people*. Chrysotom defined MAKROTHU-MIA as the spirit which could take revenge if it like, but utterly refuses to do so. I find that this characteristic is a needed quality for the pastor of a flock. Listen to the Lord's counsel to me as a Christian minister:

> . . . giving no cause for offense in anything, in order that the ministry be not discredited, but in everything commending ourselves as servants of God, in much endurance . . . in purity, in knowledge, in *patience*, in kindness . . . (2 Corinthians 6:3-4,6).

If one attempts to lead a congregation without this Spirit-given virtue, he is driven to frustration, irritability, and severity. His pulpit becomes an avenue of anger, his preaching a diatribe of demands, and his person insulting and intolerant as Diotrephes of old. God encourages me and my ilk to be "long-tempered."

But there is more. This beautiful characteristic of Christ is equally important among all christians . . . and that includes *you*, my friend. Without it, you cannot walk in a manner worthy of your calling (Ephesians 4:2; Colossians 3:12). And—you are to demonstrate it before *everyone* (1 Thessalonians 5:14). That includes children, spouses, employers, neighbors, slow drivers, people who make mistakes, senior citizens, and God! In fact, patience is a by-product of love (1 Corinthians 13:4).

If you and I were asked to name an example of this enviable quality, Job would be our man. Now I am of the opinion that he didn't sit down one day and make up his mind that he would be a patient person. Surely he never tried to bargain with God for that virtue. In fact, the term doesn't even appear in the entire book of Job—check for yourself. James 5:11, however, makes a remark about the "endurance of Job" and we know from that comment that he was one who was patient.

How did Job become a patient person? The secret is found in the original term in James 5:11, rendered "endurance." It is HUPOMONE, meaning "to abide under." Job rested and endured under the load of suffering. He determined that he would "abide under" the blast furnace of affliction regardless of its heat. The result was patience. As the slag of self-will, phony pride, stubbornness, and resentment floated to the top under the heat of heartache, grief, pain, and sorrow, patience formed—like the purifying process of raw gold. That explains why Paul says that trials and tribulations bring about patience and perseverance within us (Romans 5:3-4).

Deepening Your Roots
James 5: 7-11; Romans 5:1-5; Galatians 5:19-24

Branching Out
1. What's happening in your life right now that's trying your patience? Rather than get angry, do what Job did: abide under it.
2. Think of someone you admire for their patient spirit. As the person for advice and how he has developed that long-tempered ability.

Take Time to Be Tender

Back when I was a kid I got a bellyache that wouldn't go away. It hurt so bad I couldn't stand up straight, or sit down without increasing the pain. Finally, my folks hauled me over to a big house in west Houston where a doctor lived. He had turned the back section into his office and clinic.

It was a hot, muggy afternoon. I was scared.

The doc decided I needed a quick exam—but he really felt I was suffering from an attack of appendicitis. He had whispered that with certainty under his breath to my mom. I remember the fear that gripped me when I pictured myself having to to a big, white-brick hospital, be put to sleep, get cut on, then endure having those stitches jerked out.

Looking back, however, I really believe that "quick exam" hurt worse than the surgery the next day. The guy was rough, I mean really rough. He poked and thumped and pulled and pushed at me like I was Raggedy Andy. I was already in pain, but when old Dr. Vice Grip got through, I felt like I had been his personal punching bag. To him, I was nothing more than a ten-year-old specimen of humanity. Male, blond, slight

44

build, ninety-nine-degree temperature, with undetermined abdominal pain—and nauseated.

Never once do I recall his looking at me, listening to me, talking with me, or encouraging me in any way. Although young, I distinctly remember feeling like I bored the man—like case No. 13 that day, appendectomy No. 796 for him in his practice. And if the truth were known, an irritating interruption in his plans for nine holes later that afternoon.

Granted, a ten-year-old with a bellyache is not the greatest challenge for a seasoned physician to face . . . but his insensitivity left a lasting impression. His lack of tender caring canceled out the significance of all those neatly framed diplomas, achievements, and awards plastered across the wall. He may have been bright . . . but he was even *more* brutal.

At that painful, terrifying moment of my life, I needed more than credentials. Even as a little kid I needed compassion. A touch of kindness. A gentle, considerate, soft-spoken word of assurance. Something to cushion the blows of the man's cut-and-dried verdict, "This boy needs surgery—meet me at Memorial at five o'clock today." Over and out.

Looking back over thirty-five years. I've learned a valuable lesson: When people are hurting, they need more than an accurate analysis and diagnosis. More than professional advice. More, much more, than a stern, firm turn of a verbal wrench that cinches everything down tight.

Attorneys, doctors, counselors, physical therapists, dentists, fellow ministers, nurses, teachers, disciplers, parents, hear ye, *hear ye!* Fragile and delicate are the feelings of most who seek our help. They need to sense we are there because we care . . . not just because it's our job. Truth and tact make great bedfellows.

Sound too liberal? Weak? Would it help if you could see that someone like the Apostle Paul embraced this philosophy? He did. Although a brilliant and disciplined man, he was tender.

> You know we never used flattery, nor did we put on a mask to cover up greed—God is our witness. We were not looking for praise from men, not from you or anyone else.
>
> As apostles of Christ we could have been a burden to you, but we were gentle among you, like a mother caring for her little children. We loved you so much that we were delighted to share with you not only the gospel of God but our lives as well, because you had become so dear to us (1 Thessalonians 2:5-8 NIV).

Someday we shall all be at the receiving end—you can count on it. We shall be the ones in need of affirmation, encouragement, a gentle touch of tenderness. It's like the time-worn counsel of the good doctor Thomas Sydenham, the "English Hippocrates" (1624-1689). Addressing himself to the professionals of his day. Dr. Sydenham wrote:

> It becomes every person who purposes to give himself to the care of others, seriously to consider the four following things: First, that he must one day give an account to the Supreme Judge of all the lives entrusted to his care. Second, that all his skill and knowledge and energy, as they have been given him by God, so they should be

exercized for His glory and the good of mankind, and not for mere gain or ambition. Third, and not more beautifully than truly, let him reflect that he has undertaken the care of no mean creature; for, in order that he may estimate the value, the greatness of the human race, the only begotten Son of God became himself a man, and thus ennobled it with His divine dignity, and far more than this, died to redeem it. And fourth, that the doctor being himself a mortal human being, should be diligent and tender in relieving his suffering patients, inasmuch as he himself must one day be a like sufferer.

And that applies to ten-year-olds with a bellyache, eighty-year-olds with a backache, anybody with a headache . . . and everybody with a heartache.

Deepening Your Roots
Acts 24:23; Luke 10:25:37; Genesis 47:11-12

Branching Out
1. Find someone who's sick in bed, or in the hospital, and do some gentle caring toward him.
2. Search out and find a young child who is ill and give him some TLC.
3. When you send in that payment to your doctor or dentist, include a note of encouragement or an item that would communicate you care about his health and well-being.

Risking Liberty

There is something all of us want to be, need to be, and ought to be, but only a few really are. A very small percentage of those in God's family can honestly and boldly declare, "I am   ." Even though we think it's good and we say it's right. Even though we love its benefits and we defend its value. Though it's ours to claim, we don't. Though it's available to enjoy, we won't. It is biblically supported, theologically sound, commanded by God, and desired by man . . . but rare is the Christian who fully enters into it with enthusiasm.

What is it? *Freedom*, that's what. All of us want to be free, need to be free, ought to be free. But wait, does god really say it's OK? You decide.

> It was for freedom that Christ set us free; therefore keep standing firm and do not be subject again to a yoke of slavery (Galatians 5:1).
> For you were called to freedom, brethren (Galatians 5:013a).
> . . . and you shall know the truth, and the truth shall make you free. . . . If therefore the Son shall make you free, you shall be free indeed (John 8:32,36).
> Now the Lord is the Spirit; and where the Spirit of the Lord is, there is liberty (2 Corinthians 3:17).

48

There's more, much more. In fact, there is an entire letter in the New Testament devoted to this one subject. It's Galatians, a book of the Bible someone dubbed the "magna charta of Christian liberty." Good description. Sit down and read it soon. It is designed to set you free. It is so potent it says that those who chose to remain enslaved have (get this) "fallen from grace" (Galatians 5:4b). Wow!

Liberty and slavery, you see, are absolutely incompatible. Opposites. One is out in the open, the other behind bars.

But let's not tiptoe around with peripheral problems. Let's come to terms with our struggle with liberty. It's the *risk* involved. Misuse is another way to put it. You can hardly abuse slavery, but you certainly can liberty. Many do. Which brings up the basic questions: "With such a potential for misuse, is it really wise to teach Christians that they are free? Is it safe to tear up the man-made lists and let out the rope? Isn't it risky to promote liberty, living by grace, being free to become who we really are?

Safe? No. Risky? You'd better believe it.

The risk of liberty is that some people are bound to misuse it. And because of that, most choose the safe option and say little about freedom other than shouting, "Don't turn it into license!" Now listen—there is *always* the danger that some will do the wrong thing, the destructive thing, the sinful thing. It's like letting our teenagers go. Tossing them the keys is a risk. Every time. But the alternative is not a valid option. No kid ever grew up to become responsible and mature without mom and dad encouraging the freedom to grow.

It is, admittedly, a difficult thing to do, but preserving and promoting the freedom of the individual believer to be responsible, to make decisions, to determine choices (even wrong ones occasionally), and to live with the consequences of his actions is the key to developing a "liberty mentality" rather than an enslaved captive. We must, I repeat, we *must* encourage maturity with our brothers and sisters in the family of God. Since Christ has set us free, we dare not imprison them behind the legalistic bars of our own opinions, traditions, or personal preferences.

I read recently that the life cycle of a silkworm from egg to worm to moth includes the state at which the worm spins about itself a remarkable cocoon. This little sack is composed of 400 to 800 yards of silk fiber which seals it from the inside as it waits for metamorphosis. At the completion of the cycle, the adult mouth will break the cocoon, tearing apart the fine silk cords that bind it, and fly free. But the silkworm farmer does not allow most to become adults. At a key point in the cycle, he steams the cocoons to free, leaving a trail of broken threads which are useless to the exploiters. If they were allowed to mature and escape, by the way, the reproductive moth would lay up to 350 eggs. But they are not allowed to do so . . .

Could it be that many immature, caged Christians are kept from maturing because their ecclesiastical "captors" cannot fulfill selfish purposes in free people? Who wants their secure—though immature—traditions left behind in shambles? And we can't forget the hassle, either. Teaching people how to fly takes a lot more time and trouble than just allowing them to crawl.

A room full of moths is certainly a bigger challenge than a box full of worms.

Deepening Your Roots
1 Corinthians 9:19; 2 Corinthians 3:1-18

Branching Out
1. What keeps you from being free? Tackle one of your infringements and claim the truth: I am FREE in Christ.
2. Do you keep others from being free? Are you afraid to allow your spouse, friend, or children to make mistakes? Decide who you have the most difficulty setting free and make an effort to let them go it alone this week without your protective hand or thoughts. If they should fail, be the first to encourage them, not gloat over their mistake or say, "I told you so."

Compromise and Consequence

I don't know anyone who would like to build a summer home at the base of Mt. St. Helens. Not many would stand in line to buy real estate in Venice. It would be tough trying to get campers to pitch their tents where Big Foot had been spotted.

No family I know is interested in vacationing in a houseboat twenty feet above Niagara Falls. Or swimming in the Amazon near a school of piranhas. Or taking an evening stroll through Harlem. Or building a new home that straddles the San Andreas fault.

There's not a dad in America who'd let his daughter date a convicted murderer . . . or encourage his boy to wash windows at San Quentin.

I mean, some things make no sense at all. Like lighting a match to see if your gas tank is empty. Or stroking a rhino to see if he's tame. Man, that's lethal! They've got a name for nuts who try such stunts. Victims. Or (if they live to tell the story) just plain *stupid*.

And yet there's a strange species of Christian running loose today who flirts with risks far greater than any of the above. That's right. And they will do so with such a calm face you'd swear they had ice water in their veins. You could never guess by a glance they are balancing on the thin edge of disaster. Without a pole. And without a net.

Who are they? They are the ones who rewrite the Bible to accommodate their life-style. We've all met them. From the skin out they have all the appearance of Your Basic Believer, but down inside, operation rationalization transpires daily. They are experts at re-phrasing or explaining away the painful truth of the text.

How do they think? Well, it's not very complicated. Whenever they run across Scripture verses or principles that attack their position, they alter them to accomodate their practice. That way, two things occur:

1. All desires (no matter how wrong) are fulfilled.
2. All guilt (no matter how justified) is erased.

That way everybody can do his own thing and nobody has any reason to question anybody's action. If he does, call him a legalist and low right on. Oh yeah, you've gotta talk a lot about grace, too. That helps to spook the bunch who would otherwise criticize.

What are some examples? Just look around and listen. Here is a sampling of accommodating theology:

- *God wants me to be happy. I can't be happy married to her. So I'm leaving . . . and I know He'll understand.*
- *There was a time when this might have been considered immoral. But not today. The Lord gave me this desire and wants me to enjoy it.*
- *Look, nobody's perfect. So I got in deeper than I planned. Sure, it's a little shady, but what's grace all about, anyway?*
- *Me? Ask His forgiveness? That's ridiculous. My re-*

lationship with God is much deeper than shallow techniques like that.

- *Hey, if it feels good, have at it! Life's too short to sweat small stuff. We're not under law, you know.*
- *So what if a little hanky-panky . . . a little fun 'n' games goes on? What's life about without some spice and risk? All those 'thou shalt nots' are unrealistic*

If that's true . . . if that's right, then what in the world does it mean to be *holy?*

As obedient children, do not be conformed to the former lusts which were yours in your ignorance, but like the Holy One who called you, be holy yourselves also in all your behavior; because it is written, ''You shall be holy, for I am holy'' (1 Peter 1:14-16).

Or *pure?*

For this is the will of God, your sanctification; that is, that you abstain from seual immorality. . . . abstain from every form of evil (1 Thessalonians 4:3, 5:22).

Or *under grace?*

What then? Shall we sin because we are not under law but under grace? May it never be? (Romans 6:15).

Or *undefiled?*

Let marriage be held in honor among all, and let the marriage be undefiled; for fornicators and adulterers God will judge (Hebrews 13:4).

The simple fact is this: We reap *precisely* what we sow. If we sow a lifestyle that is more comfortable or easier or even happier—but is in direct disobedience to God's revealed Word—we intimately reap *disaster*.

Do not be deceived, God is not mocked; for whatever a man sows, this he will also reap. For the one who sows to his own flesh and shall from the flesh reap corruption . . . (Galatians 6:7-8a).

It may not come soon . . . but it will come. And when it does, no one will have to explain what it means to be holy, pure, under grace, or undefiled. When the bills come due, the wages of willful sin are paid in full. God may seem slow, but He doesn't compromise with consequences.

Deepening Your Roots
Leviticus 18:1-30; Galatians 3:1-14; Ephesians 5:1-11; 1 Thessalonians 4:1-7

Branching Out
1. Confide in a Christian friend you trust and ask him to help you overcome a sin you keep repeating.
2. Memorize a verse from Scripture that will help you choose right the next time you're confronted with a temptation or want to rationalize.
3. Get serious. Ask God to help you overcome an area of your life you know isn't godly. If you're not ready to ask God for help, then ask Him to help you become convicted about it.

Worm Theology

Ever get a song on your mind? Sure, it happens to everyone. It can drive you crazy . . . like a silly commercial jingle. The Madison Avenue guy makes them that way—so they'll stick like cockleburs to a spaniel's ear. Sometimes, however, the melody on the brain is a welcome one. Like a solid, old hymn that keeps us company during a lonely afternoon.

It happened to me last week. Isaac Watts struck again. One of his best (he wrote over 600!) lingered in my head for more than an hour before I actually formed the words with my mouth. Suddenly, I found myself listening to what Watts wrote over two centuries ago:

> Alas! and did my Savior bleed?
> And did my Sovereign die?
> Would He devote that sacred Head
> For such a worm as I?

I frowned as that last line faded away: "A worm"? Does God see people as "worms"? When Christ died did He "devote that sacred head" for *worms*? Now, obviously, Watts wanted to portray a vivid illustration of sinful mankind—lost, undeserving, spiritually worthless, wicked within. Dipping his brush in Job 25 and Isaiah 41, the hymnist painted such a picture, using the very term Scripture uses—*worm*. He was biblical and therefore justified in his choice of terms for the text. Frankly, we were worm-like when our righteous God found us—lowly, wandering, dirty, unattractive, grubby creatures.

But that doesn't mean we work hard at making ourselves into worms now. *A child of God is not a worm.* If God had wanted you to be a worm, He could have very easily made you one! He's very good at worms, you know. There's an infinite variety of the wriggly creatures. When Watts wrote of worms, he was merely using a word picture. Many others, however, have framed it as a model to follow, calling it humility. This ''worm theology'' creates enormous problems.

It wears many faces—all sad. It crawls out from between the mattress and the springs in the morning, telling itself, ''I'm nothing. I'm a worm. Woe, woe. I can't do anything and even if I appear to be doing something, it's not really me. Woe! I must annihilate self-respect . . . crucify all motivation and ambition. If any good accidentally leaks out, I must quickly hide it or categorically deny I had anything to do with it. How could *I* accomplish anything of value? I mean, who am I? I'm a worm. Good for nothing except crawling very slowly, drowning in mud puddles, or getting stepped on. Woe, woe, woe.''

There's one main problem with this sort of thinking—*it's phony*. No matter how diligently we labor to appear genuinely humble, it amounts to nothing more than trying to look good in another way. Self-made worms carry around little signs you have to squint at to read:

I bet I'm twice as humble as you.

And therein lies the ugly sin: PRIDE.

Heretical though it may sound, no one who actually hates himself can adequately share the love of Christ. Our Lord taught that we were to love our neighbors *as we love ourselves*. Think that over. If we don't properly love ourselves, where does that leave our neighbors? I have yet to witness an effective, happy, fulfilled Christian whose image of himself was poor . . . who *really* believed he was a worm.

Have you taken time this week to consider before your Lord and His Word who you really are? It's impossible to imagine that one who is adopted into God's family, accepted in the Beloved, a recipient of the riches of Christ, called to be His ambassador, and the object of infinite grace, mercy, love, and peace, ought to either around like a nightcrawler. If you ask me, *that's* heresy!

Sinful? Oh yes. Underserving? Absolutely. Imperfect? Who isn't? Selfish? Indeed! Wrong? More often than not.

But a *worm?* Useless? Unimportant? Spineless? Meaningless? No, not that. God declared us righteous. He lifted us out of the miry clay and set us upon a rock. He invites us to approach Him with boldness. And He means it!

No condemnation now I dread;
Jesus, and all in Him is mine!
Alive in Him, my living Head,

And clothed in righteousness Divine.
Bold, I approach the eternal throne,
And claim the crown, through Christ my own.

Now *there's* a song to get stuck in your mind.

Deepening Your Roots
Job 25:1-5; Psalm 8:1-9; Isaiah 41:14-16; Romans 3:21-26; Hebrews 4:16

Branching Out
1. Do something for yourself today that brings you happiness. As you do it, remind yourself that "you're important, too!"
2. Do something for your neighbor that you would like your neighbor to do for you.
3. Memorize a song you sing at church. Let it get stuck in your mind.

Failures

Snake River Canyon coiled up, rattled its tail, and sank its fangs into its would-be captor. On a sultry Sunday afternoon its 1,700-foot jaws yawned wide as it swallowed a strange-tasting capsule prescribed for it by Dr. Robert C. Truax, the scientist-designer of *Sky Cycle X-2*. Starring in the show was a guy some people tagged Captain Marvel, who looked more like Billy Batson unable to remember the magic word. But before we label him a showman . . . or a show-off . . . I suggest we consider the outcome of this showdown.

Any third grader could have told you the vaunted skycycle leap across the canyon was a triple-A flop—a classic fizzle. The skycycle gave up in mid-air; the driver floated to safety beneath a nylon cloud. But you won't find him sitting long-faced in a dark corner today. Most people send an ambulance and a wrecker to mop up their mistakes. He could have sent a Brink's armored car. As bystanders shouted "Rip off!" he was thinking about write-offs. Anyone who can walk away from a failure with a smile, a bulging rear pocket, and his pride still intact has to have *something* going for him. The real six-million dollar man, if you can believe it, is a two-wheeled wonder named Evel Knievel. Nobody—but *nobody* in the long history of sports ever came off a more abysmal failure better than he. The remains of Dr. Truax's flopcycle littered the canyon, but the man who took off like a bird made out like a banker.

When you stop and think it over, there's an abiding truth in that Idaho extravaganza all of us ought to capture and cultivate. It's much greater than money and far deeper than a canyon jump. There's a philosophy of life here I'm now convinced is worth one's pursuit. Here it is:

THE PERSON WHO SUCCEEDS IS NOT THE ONE
WHO HOLDS BACK, FEARING FAILURE, NOR
THE ONE WHO NEVER FAILS . . . BUT RATHER
THE ONE WHO MOVES ON IN SPITE OF FAILURE.

As Lowell wrote:
  Not failure, but low aim, is crime.
As Teddy Roosevelt believed:

Far better it is to dare mighty things, to win glorious triumphs, even though checkered by failure, than to take rank with those poor spirits who neither enjoy much nor suffer much because they live in the gray twilight that knows neither victory nor defeat.

Give me a "skycycle" and a 108-foot take-off ramp with all its risks any day—before you sentence me to the path of predictability between the stone walls of routine and fear. God asks that we believe Him *regardless* of the risks—in spite of the danger—ignoring the odds. The ancient city of Jericho was defeated because Joshua and his troops defied the "normal procedure" of battle . . . never once fearing failure. The

Gentiles heard of Christ Jesus because Paul and a few companions kept getting back up after being knocked down. Peter's two letters are in the Book because he refused to live in the shadow of his bad track record.

Great accomplishments are often attempted but only occasionally reached. What is interesting (and encouraging) is that those who reach them are usually those who missed many times before. Failures, you see, are only temporary tests to prepare us for permanent triumphs.

Whoever you are today—listen to me! Sitting there licking your wounds will only result in a bitter aftertaste. Sighs and tears and thoughts of quitting are understandable for the moment but *inexcusable* for the future. Get up and get on with it!

And if you're looking for an absolute guarantee against future failures, I know of only one—death.

Deepening Your Roots
Joshua 6:1-27; 1 Samuel 17:1-50; 1 Chronicles 11:15-19

Branching Out
1. Start doing something that you've put off because of the risk of failure.
2. Make a meal tonight using two new recipes. Take the risk.
3. Go to a local ice cream parlor and try a flavor you've never had.

The Broken Wing

It is quite probable that someone reading my words this moment is fighting an inner battle with a ghost from the past. The skeleton is one of yesterday's closets is beginning to rattle louder and louder. Putting adhesive tape around the closet and moving the bureau in front of the door does little to muffle the clattering bones. You wonder, possibly, "Who knows?" You think, probably, "I've had it . . . can't win . . . party's over."

The anchor that tumbled off your boat is dragging and snagging on the bottom. Guilt and anxiety have come aboard, pointing out the great dark hulks of shipwrecks below. They busy themselves drilling worryholes in your hull and you are beginning to sink. Down in the hold, you can hear them chant an old lie as they work: "The bird with the broken pinion never soared as high again . . ."

Allow me to present a case in opposition to these destructive and inaccurate accusers. It may be true that you've done or experienced things which would embarrass you if they became public knowledge. You may have committed a terrible and tragic sin that was never traced back to you. You may have a criminal record or a moral charge or a domestic conflict that, to this moment, is private information. You may wrestle with a past that has been fractured and wounded by a mental or emotional breakdown. Futile attempts at suicide may add to the previous scar tissue and increase your fear of being labeled ''sick'' or ''nervous.'' It is possible that you live with memories, covered now by the sands of time, of an illicit relationship or a financial failure or a terrible habit or a divorce or a scandalous involvement. You feel that any one of these things might mar or cripple your reputation if the dirty details on the table of gluttonous gossipers.

But wait a minute. Before you surrender your case as hopeless, consider the liberating evidence offered in the Bible. Take an honest look at men and women whom God used *in spite* of their past! *Abraham,* founder of Israel and tagged ''the friend of God,'' was once a worshiper of idols. *Joseph* had a prison record but later became prime minister of Egypt. *Moses* was a murderer, but later became the one who delivered his nation from the slavery of Pharaoh. *Jephthah* was an illegitimate child who ran around with a tough bunch of hoods before he was chosen by God to become His personal representative. *Rahab* was a harlot in the streets of Jericho but was later used in such a mighty way that God enlisted her among the members of His hall of fame in Hebrews 11.

Still unconvinced? There's more. *Eli* and *Samuel* were both poor, inconsistent fathers, but proved to be strong men in God's hand regardless. *Jonah* and *John Mark* were missionaries who ran away from hardship like cowards but were ever-so-profitable later on. *Peter* openly denied the Lord and cursed Him, only to return and become God's choicest spokesman among the early years of the infant church. *Paul* was so hard and vicious in his early life the disciples and apostles refused to believe he'd actually become a Christian . . . but you know how greatly God used him. We could go on and on. The files of heaven are filled with stories of re-deemed, refitted renegades and rebels.

How magnificent is grace! How malignant is guilt! How sweet are the promises! How sour is the past! How precious and broad is God's love! How petty and narrow are man's limitations! How refreshing is the Lord! How rigid is the legalist!

There is not a single saint in a single church free from a few things he or she is ashamed of—not one of us! The one who thinks otherwise is worse than all the rest combined. In plain, garden-variety English, we were all taken from the same dunghill. And so we all fight the same fight with the filth of the flesh regardless of how loudly we sing, how piously we pray, or how sweetly we say hello.

Mark it—when God forgives, He forgets. He is not only willing but pleased to use any vessel—just as long as it is clean *today*. It may be cracked or chipped. It may be worn or it may have never been used before. You can count on this—the past ended one second ago. From this point onward, you can be clean, filled with His Spirit, and used in many different ways for His honor. God's glorious grace says: "Throw guilt and anxiety overboard . . . draw the anchor . . . trim the sails . . . man the rudder . . . a strong gale is coming!"

Deepening Your Roots
Daniel 9:4-19; Luke 7:36-48; Acts 10:34-43

Branching Out
1. In celebration of God's forgiveness towards you, be the first to forget and forgive an action your spouse or friend did to you.
2. Look through your garage and try to come up with an old clay pot that has a crack or two in it. Set it on the kitchen counter or in a place where you'll see it often. Leave it there for a week and let it remind you of the fact that God delights in using us. His vessels, no matter how ''weak'' we are.

Searching for Shelter

Discouragement.

Where does it come from?

Sometimes it feels like a dry, barren wind off a lonely desert. And something inside us begins to wilt.

At other times it feels like chilling mist. Seeping through our pores, it numbs the spirit and fogs the path before us.

What is it about discouragement that strips our lives of joy and leaves us feeling vulnerable and exposed?

I don't know all the reasons. I don't even know most of the reasons. But I do know *one* of the reasons: We don't have a refuge. Shelters are hard to come by these days . . . you know, people who care enough to listen. Who are good at keeping secrets. And we all need harbors to pull into when we feel weather-worn and blasted by the storm.

I have an old Marine buddy who became a Christian several years after he was discharged from the Corps. When news of his conversion reached me, I was pleasantly surprised. He was one of those guys you'd never picture as being interested in spiritual things. He cursed loudly, drank heavily, fought hard, chased women, loved weapons, and hated chapel service. *He was a great marine*. But God? They weren't on speaking terms when I bumped around with him.

Then one day we ran into each other. As the conversation turned to his salvation, he frowned, put his hand on my shoulder, and admitted:

"Chuck, the only thing I miss is that old fellowship all the guys in our outfit used to have down at the slop shoot (Greek for tavern on base). Man, we'd sit around, laugh, tell stories, drink a few beers, and really let our hair down. It was great! I just haven't found anything to take the place of that great time we used to enjoy. I ain't got nobody to admit my faults to . . . to have 'em put their arms around me and tell me I'm still okay."

My stomach churned. Not because I was shocked, but because I had to agree. The man needed a refuge . . . someone to hear him out. The incident reminded me of something I read several months ago:

> The neighborhood bar is possibly the best counterfeit there is to the fellowship Christ wants to give His church. It's an imitation, dispensing liquor instead of grace, escape rather than reality, but it is a permissive, accepting, and inclusive fellowship. It is unshockable. It is democratic. You can tell people secrets and they usually don't tell others or even want to. The bar flourishes not because most people are alcoholics, but because God has put into the human heart the desire to know and be known, to love and be loved, and so many seek a counterfeit at the price of a few beers.
>
> With all my heart I believe that Christ wants His church to be . . . a fellowship where people can come in and say, "I'm sunk!" "I've had it!"[4]

Let me get painfully specific. Where do *you* turn when the bottom drops out of *your* life? Or when you face an issue that is embarrassing . . . maybe even scandalous. Like:

- You just discovered your son is a practicing homosexual.
- Your mate is talking separation or divorce.
- Your daughter has run away . . . for the fourth time . . . and you're afraid she's pregnant.
- You've lost your job. It's your own fault.
- Financially, you've blown it.
- Your parent is an alcoholic.
- Your wife is having an affair.
- You flunked your entrance exam or you messed up the interview.
- You're in jail because you broke the law.

What do you need when circumstances puncture your fragile dikes and threaten to engulf your life with pain and confusion?

You need a shelter. A listener. Someone who understands.

But to whom do you turn when there's no one to tell your troubles to? Where do you find encouragement?

Without preaching, I'd like to call to your attention a man who turned to the living Lord and found in Him a place to rest and repair. His name? David. Cornered, bruised by adversity, and struggling with a low self-esteem, he wrote these words in his journal of woes:

> In you, O LORD, I have taken refuge;
>> let me never be put to shame;
>> deliver me in your righteousness.
> Turn your ear to me,
>> come quickly to my rescue;

> be my rock of refuge,
> a strong fortress to save me (Psalm 31:1-2 NIV).

Failing in strength and wounded in spirit, David cries out his need for a "refuge." The Hebrew term speaks of a protective place, a place of safety, security, secrecy. he tells the Lord that He—Jehovah God—became his refuge. In Him the troubled man found encouragement.

Now the question: Why do we need a refuge? As I read on through this psalm, I find three reasons unfolding:

First, because we are in distress and sorrow accompanies us.

> Be merciful to me, O LORD, for I am in distress;
> my eyes grow weak with sorrow,
> my soul and my body with grief.
> My life is consumed by anguish (vv. 9:10a NIV).

Eyes get red from weeping. The heavy weights of sorrow press down. Depression, that serpent of despair, slithers silently through the soul's back door.

> Depression is
> Debilitating, defeating,
> Deepening gloom.
>
> Trudging wearily through
> The grocery store,
> Unable to make a simple choice,
> Or to count out correct change.
>
> Surveying an unbelievably messy house,

70

Piles of laundry,
Work undone, and not being
Able to lift a finger.

Doubting that God cares,
Doubting in my prayers,
Doubting He's even there.

Sitting, staring wild-eyed into space,
Desperately wanting out of the human race.[5]

Heavy! But that's why we need a refuge.
Second, because we are sinful and guilt accuses us.

My strength fails because of my guilt
   and my bones grow weak (v. 10b NIV).
There is shame between these lines.
Embarrassment. "It's my fault." What tough words to
choke out! "I'm to blame."
An old British minister says it all when he writes:

This is the bitterest of all—to know that suffering need
not have been; that it is the harvest of one's own sowing;
that the vulture which feeds on the vitals is a nestling of
one's own rearing. Ah me! This is pain.![6]

Harried and haunted by self-inflicted sorrow, we desperately search for a place to hide. But perhaps the most
devastating blow of all is dealt by others.

Third, because we are surrounded by adversaries and
misunderstanding assaults us.

Because of all my enemies, I am the utter contempt of
my neighbors;
I am a dread to my friends—
   those who see me on the street flee from me.

I am forgotten by them as though I were dead;
    I have become like broken pottery.
For I hear the slander of many;
    there is terror on every side;
they conspire against me
    and plot to take my life (vv. 11-13 NIV).

See how the hurting is handled?

"Utter contempt . . . a dread . . . those who see me flee from me . . . I am forgotten . . . I hear slander . . . there is terror . . . they conspire against me. . . ." Sound like a page out of your journal?

Tortured by the whisperings of others, we feel like a wounded, bleeding mouse in the paws of a hungry cat. The thought of what people are saying is more than we can bear. Gossip (even its name hisses) gives the final shove as we strive for balance at the ragged edge of despair.

Discouraged people don't need critics. They hurt enough already. They don't need more guilt or piled-on distress. They need encouragement. They need a refuge.

A place to hide and heal.

A willing, caring, available someone. A confident and comrade-at-arms. Can't find one? Why not share David's shelter? The One he called My Strength, Mighty Rock, Fortress, Stronghold, and High Tower.

David's Refuge *never* failed. Not even once. And he never regretted the times he dropped his heavy load and ran for cover.

Neither will you.

Deepening Your Roots
Psalm 18:1-3, 16-19; Psalm 32:6-7; Psalm 71:1-3

Branching Out
1. When you hear of, or are with, someone who has failed, don't criticize—be a refuge. Be forgiving and loving by listening to him and holding him with your arms of comfort.
2. Don't whisper gossip today about anyone! And don't listen to someone else's gossip either!
3. When you hear of the difficulty or failure of someone else, don't stay away. Keep being a friend and find a way to be a refuge to the person.

Manipulation

When C.S. Lewis was a student at Oxford, he made a number friends, some of whom became lifelong companions. Several in that close circle went off to become authors, like Lewis himself. Over the years, they loved to get together to talk and to read to each other their works in progress. These sessions never failed to hone and shape their thinking. Among the group were Nevill Coghill and Owen Barfield, men who were cultivating the literary craft . . . but in no way as prolific or as profound as their friend. Lewis's reputation soon eclipsed them all. The ink flowed from his pen much more rapidly than theirs, and at increasingly shorter intervals, old Clive Staples was producing meaningful materials for the world to read. This could have driven a wedge between them, but he didn't let that happen.

The more popular scholar seemed to appreciate more than ever his long-standing friends. Not once did they sense that Lewis desired to control them. Barfield once admitted:

> I never recall a single remark, a single word or silence, a single look . . . which would go to suggest that he felt his opinion was entitled to more respect than that of old

friends. I wonder how many famous men there have been of whom this could truthfully be said.

An absence of manipulation. No interest in pushing for his own way or putting down others, or in using his role or record of achievement as a subtle yet forceful lever.

Manipulation is the attempt to control, obligate, or take advantage of others by unfair or insidious means. It is practiced by insecure people who are attempting to look superior by making others squirm. Oh, it isn't usually done in a bold, up-front manner, but rather indirectly, obliquely. By little hints. Or well-timed comments. Or facial expressions.

The *Take-Charge Manipulator* is one type. This is the individual who has to come out smarter or stronger than you in order to be happy with you around. To see if you fit into this category, answer the following questions:

1. Do I drop hints that signal I know more about what's being discussed than those in charge?
2. Do I enjoy correcting factual errors in conversation?
3. Do I control an argument, looking for ways to show that the other person is at fault?
4. Do I make others feel guilty when I want a certain action?

The *Poor-Me Manipulator* is the opposite extreme. This individual attempts to get his or her way by appearing weak. After all, who can hit you while you're down and helpless? These people "clutch" at you, using sighs, tears, sickness, even depression to gain control and get their way. They love the role of *victim*, which seldom fails to arouse sympathy. Wives and husbands are great at this. So are kids! We can appear so needy, so ill . . . until we see it's not working. Then it's amazing how much energy we can muster as anger replaces weakness.

The *I-Must-Be-Needed Manipulator* is yet another type. This person is not so much one to clutch and cling, but rather to cultivate an obligation. The mother (or mother-in-law) with grown children has to deal with this, especially if she isn't employed, gets her housework done by 9:00 A.M., and is bored. Her phone rings and it's a married daughter who shares a problem she is struggling with. Mama is in her car and on her way over before the gal on the other end of the line has hung up. She steps in and gets things rolling (just like the old days!) without even being invited. Let her daughter get a little resentful and the poor-me syndrome gets set in motion, like fast . . . "Well, how ungrateful can you be, young lady!" With a slam she stomps out like a little girl who had her doll snatched away.

Manipulation is an infantile technique and yet it is practiced mainly by adults. No profession is immune. Pastors can easily resort to it, using the Bible as their defense. Physicians can rely on it as well, practicing behind the cover of the untouchable brotherhood. So can attorneys who know how to read "legalese" and secretly enjoy the power of intimidation. Or the teacher who possesses the ultimate lever—*the grade book.*

Once again our Example stands tall. Although deity in flesh, not once did He take unfair advantage of finite men and women who spent time with Him. Although Himself omniscient, He gave others room to learn, to express themselves . . . even when they were dead wrong and He could have silenced them. Never once did our Lord maneuver simply to gain the upper hand or to come out smelling like a rose. With wisdom He held His power in check and yet on those few occasions when He did release it, the purpose was to glorify God, never to manipulate man.

Paul picked up the same style from his Master. Why, he had sufficient authority to get what he wanted without even saying "please." A snap of his fingers would have brought food to his table or put shekels in his pocket. No way! He simply refused to throw his apostolic weight around.

> Never once did we try to win you with flattery, as you very well know, and God knows we were not just pretending to be your friends so that you would give us money! As for praise, we have never asked for it from you or anyone else, although as apostles of Christ we certainly had a right to some honor from you (1 Thessalonians 2:5-6 TLB).

If you are in a position of authority, no matter how small or how large, the temptation to manipulate will never go away. You may have the authority to claim certain honors . . . to call attention to your right to be listened to. You may even be encouraged to do so by well-meaning devotees who want to see you get ahead. Don't yield. Resist at all cost.

If C.S. Lewis could restrain with all his brilliance, popularity, and record of achievements, so can we. There's a word for those who shun this counsel and push people around to get their way.

Lonely.

Deepening Your Roots
Genesis 27:1-35; Luke 4:1-12; 1 Thessalonians 2:1-16

Branching Out
1. Next time you sense someone manipulating you, graciously confront the person with how you feel. Learn from the experience by storing in your mind how being manipulated made you feel.
2. Give someone a note before your next business meeting, or family gathering, and ask the individual to observe you, watching for any manipulative comments or actions.

Disorientation

Right now I'm looking at a cartoon that portrays a disheveled, stubble-faced, pajama-clad man who has evidently just thrown back the covers of his bed and put his warm feet on the cold door. "On Monday mornings," he mumbles, "I don't know if I'm alive or on tape."

Now there's a guy I can identify with! Reminds me of the story President Harry Truman enjoyed telling. A man was hit on the head at work. The blow was so severe he was knocked unconscious for an extended period of time. His family, convinced he was dead, called the funeral home and asked the local undertaker to pick him up at the hospital, which he did. Early the following morning this dear man suddenly awoke and sat straight up in the casket. Confused, he blinked several times and looked around, trying to put the whole thing together. He thought:

"If I'm alive, what in the world am I doing in this soft, satin-filled box? And if I'm dead, why do I have to go to the bathroom?"

Disorientation is the pits. When you travel a lot (like airline personnel) you have to deal with it. When you fight deadlines as days run into nights (like tax consultants and publishing editors) you have to work out ways to cope with it. When you are confined to tight places of inescapable spaces (like astronauts or prisoners or victims of confining illnesses)—again, that old bug-a-boo is there to ready to bite, leaving you in the wake of depression or one of its emotional relatives.

I find it also happens after extremely busy times in my life. While the dust is flying and activities are happening and decisions are occurring and plans are unfolding, we sorta tie a knot and hang on. We keep thinking that soon it will be over and things will return to normal. But ''normal,'' when it finally happens, seems strange, almost unmanageable. This is never more emphatic than when people ''retire'' from their occupations which have kept them in touch and needed all their adult lives. Abruptly—after a brief flurry of farewells, thank-yous, nice words, and a gold watch—that individual feels put out to pasture. Out of touch. No longer needed. Life is strangely reduced to fading memories, an abstruse existence sandwiched between the foggy feelings of uselessness and loss of identity.

I watched my own father cave in after he retired, as disorientation replaced definitive living. His sense of humor soon lost its keen edge. His once-adventurous spirit turned to restlessness. He talked less, he traveled less, and, what's worse—he *thought* less. Not because he was without money or without health . . . but because he was without purpose. And without close friends. And without the plant superintendent giving him a to-do list every day as he showed up (always forty-five minutes early). No longer was there a shop whistle at quitting time or the grinding sounds of a turret lathe as dark-blue chips of steel screamed while being stripped away. Now all was quiet. Desperately quiet. Maddeningly quiet. Not even television could fill the void. And it wasn't twelve months before the thief of senility began to steal away the man's drive. Oh, he lived many, many years beyond sixty-five. But most of those years, I'm saddened to say, were marked by tragic disorientation.

Why bother you with all this? Why worry about such a distant dilemma in this day of circus-like atmosphere and a schedule that would fatigue a rhino? Well, as Solomon once said,

> . . . Because childhood and the prime of life are fleeting (Ecclesiastes 11:10).

And because there may be a time when

> . . . the years draw near when you will say, "I have no delight in them" (Ecclesiastes 12:1).

You see, there's nothing in the Bible that says none of that will happen before you "retire." Monday morning blues are not restricted to folks in Leisure World. Disorientation is not a cloud that floats only over Sun City. Nor is it limited to Vietnam vets or inmates at a camp in Siberia.

Wanna fight it? Make and cultivate a few very close friends. Stay in touch with people. Give of yourself. Read widely. Exercise regularly and strenuously. Turn the TV off. Fight the rut of routine. Leave time for leisure. Have more fun. Take up a hobby or pastime that gets you outdoors. Don't let your occupation enslave you. Eat less. Laugh more. Quit fussing. Encourage at least one person every day. Stop living for money. Plant a garden. Replace fake plants with real ones in your home. Trust God for something that seems impossible. Loosen up your intensity. Stop taking yourself (and your kids) so seriously. Start today.

Yesterday was Monday. I went sailing with a friend. It was great therapy out on the blue Pacific. Today is Tuesday. I'm looking forward to Wednesday and Thursday and even Friday because I pulled out all the stops on Monday. I may even preach better on Sunday because I sailed last Monday . . . but I wouldn't bet on it.

On Monday I was live, but everything on Sunday is taped.

Deepening Your Roots
Numbers 8:20-25; 1 Kings 2:1-11; Luke 19:11-26

Branching Out
1. Do something this week that you've never done before.
2. Encourage one person every day this week.

Relaying the Truth

It was late afternoon when the boat's engine sputtered, stalled, and refused to restart. Gallons of water surged into the craft as it pitched on sickening, six-foot swells. The five Jaegers had done all they knew to do, but it wasn't enough. An exciting fishing trip was now a thing of horror. They were going under.

Grim-faced, George Jaeger, his three sons, and his elderly father methodically tightened the buckles on their life jackets, tied themselves together with a rope, and slipped silently into a black and boiling Atlantic.

George glanced at his watch as the boat finally disappeared—6:30 P.M. Very little was said. It grew dark. First one boy and then another swallowed too much salt water, gagged, and strangled on the brine as they fought to keep their heads up. The helpless father heard his sons, one by one, then his dad, choke and drown. But George couldn't surrender. After eight nightmarish hours, he staggered onto the shore, still pulling the rope that bound him to the bodies of the other four. Pause to try and imagine the sight!

"I realized they were all dead—my three boys and my father—but I guess I didn't want to accept it, so I kept swimming all night long," he later told reporters.

"My youngest boy, Clifford, was the first to go. I had always taught our children not to fear death because it was being with Jesus Christ." Before Cliff died, his dad heard him say, "I'd rather be with Jesus than go on fighting."

In that vivid Atlantic memory, George Jaeger had a chance to witness the impact of his fifteen years as a father. The boys died quietly, with courage and dignity. Up to the very last minute, one by one they modeld the truth passed on by their father: When under pressure, stay calm . . . think . . . even if death is near, keep under control. So they did and so they died. When the ultimate test was administered in an angry sea, they handed in perfect scores.

In her bestseller, *What Is a Family?* Edith Schaeffer devotes her longest chapter to the idea that a family is a *perpetual relay of truth*. A place where principles are hammered and honed on the anvil of everyday living. Where character traits are sculptured under the watchful eyes of moms and dads. Where steel-strong fibers are woven into the fabric of inner constitution.

The relay place. A race with a hundred batons.

> *Determination.* "Stick with it, regardless."
> *Honesty.* "Speak and live the truth—always."
> ● *Responsibility.* "Be dependable, be trustworthy."
> *Thoughtfulness.* "Think of others before yourself."
> *Confidentiality.* "Don't tell secrets. Seal your lips."
> *Punctuality.* "Be on time."
> *Self-control.* "When under stress, stay calm."
> *Patience.* "Fight irritability. Be willing to wait."

- *Purity.* "Reject anything that lowers your standards."
- *Compassion.* "When another hurts, feel it with him."
- *Diligence.* "Work hard. Tough it out."

And how is this done? Over the long haul, believe me. This race is not a sprint, it's a marathon. There are no fifty-yard dash courses on character building. Relays require right timing and smooth hand-offs—practiced around the track hour after hour when nobody is looking. And where is this practice track? Where is this place where rough edges cannot remain hidden, must not be left untouched? Inside your own front door. *The home* is God's built-in training facility.

That's why He urged all the dads in Moses' day to relay the truth:

> . . . and you shall teach them diligently to your sons and shall talk of them when you sit in your house and when you walk by the way and when you lie down and when you rise up (Deuteronomy 6:7).

That's the plan—the inimitable strategy which makes winners out of runners. Relay the truth—diligently, consistently. One final warning, however. If you determine to make this your goal, you'll have to outdistance two relentless foes: slow starts and sloppy handoffs. Keep in mind, moms and dads, you really don't have forever. Negligence will catch you from behind and beat you in the stretch if you let up. And don't think your kids will let you get away with faking it, either.

I just read about a salesman who knocked on the door of a rundown apartment house in a low-rent district. The mother didn't want to talk to the guy, so she told her little boy to tell him she couldn't come to the door because she was in the bathtub. Her son answered the door this way: "We ain't got no bathtub, but Mom told me to tell you she's in it."

Furthermore, it won't work for you to play catch-up by dumping a truckload of truth once or twice a year. The secret of good parenting is consistency. Never forget that.

Got the game plan, now? Stay at it, day in and day out. And make sure your handoffs are crisp and sharp throughout this race against time. Relays are won or lost at that critical moment when a young hand reaches back and gropes for the baton.

Ask George Jaeger.

Deepening Your Roots
Deuteronomy 6:4-9; Luke 2:21-51

Branching Out
1. Talk to at least one of your children or a friend about death.
2. Ask your kids, or a friend you respect, to name one way you are inconsistent. Don't defend yourself. Rather, accept their observation as truth and work on changingit.
3. Pick an activity and do it at the exact same time for the five days in a row. Evaluate your consistency, or inconsistency.

God's Control

The bitter news of Dawson Trotman's drowning swept like cold wind across Schroon Lake to the shoreline. Eyewitnesses tell of the profound anxiety, the tears, the helpless disbelief in the faces of those who now looked out across the deep blue water. Everyone's face except one—Lila Trotman, Dawson's widow. As she suddenly walked upon the scene a close friend shouted, "Oh, Lila . . . he's gone. Dawson's gone!" To that she replied in calm assurance the words of Psalm 115:3:

> But our God is in the heavens;
> He does whatever he pleases.

All of the anguish, the sudden loneliness that normally consumes and cripples those who survive did not invade that woman's heart. Instead, she leaned hard upon her sovereign Lord.

As you read these words . . . does that seem strange to you? Does it seem unusual to refer to a tragic death as being God's pleasure? Honestly now, do you think God's control over us is total . . . or partial? Let's allow His Word to speak on this deep subject:

Thou hast enclosed me behind and before,

And laid Thy hand upon me.
Thine eyes have sen my unformed substance;
And in Thy book they were all written,
The days that were ordained for me,
When as yet there was not one of them
(Psalm 139:5,16).

Woe to the one who quarrels with his Maker—
An earthenware vessel among the vessels of earth!
Will the day say to the potter, "What are you doing?"
(Isaiah 45:9).

. . . I am God, and there is no other;
I am God, and there is no one like Me . . .
Saying, "My purpose will be established,
And I will accomplish all My good pleasure"
(Isaiah 46:9-10).

. . . He does according to His will in the host of heaven
And among the inhabitants of earth;
And no one can ward off His hand
Or say to Him, "What hast Thou done?"
(Daniel 4:35).

There are more. Patiently, repeatedly, in a dozen different ways the Word makes the point. Accept it or not, God's calling the shots. He's running the show. Either He's in *full* control or He's off His throne. It's as foolish to say He's "almost sovereign" as it would be to say I'm "almost married" or Kennedy was "almost president" or the surgeon's gloves are "almost sterile."

If you're trying to grasp all the ramifications of this great truth . . . don't. You can't anyway. Feverishly toiling to unravel all the knots can turn you into a fanatical freak . . . it will push you to the edge of your mental capacity . . . it will result in endless hours of theological hairsplitting. The finite can *never* plumb the depths of the infinite . . . so don't waste your time trying.

It was a glorious day when I was liberated from the concentration camp of fear . . . the fear of saying, "I don't understand the reasons why, but I accept God's hand in what has happened." It was a *greater* day when I realized that nobody expected me to have all the answers . . . least of all God! If I could figure it all out, I'd qualify as His adviser, and Scripture makes it clear He doesn't need my puny counsel. He wants my unreserved love, my unqualified devotion, my undaunted trust—not my unenlightened analysis of His ways.

One of the marks of spiritual maturity is the quiet confidence that God is in control . . . without the need to understand why He does what He does. Lila Trotman bore such a mark as she faced the ways of God that were "unsearchable . . . and unfathomable."

What marks *your* life?

Deepening Your Roots?
Isaiah 45:5-9; Isaiah 46:8-11; Daniel 5:18-21

Branching Out
1. Do you remember an event or struggle during the past year when you decided to trust God? Are you glad you did? Why?
2. Ask God to reveal (sometime during the day) an area you're controlling that needs to be turned over to Him.

Very Thin Wires

I recall a phrase from one of Alexander Whyte's works. It came to mind early this morning. The old biographer wrote of our tendency

> ". . . *to hang every heavy weights on very thin wires.*"

We really do.

We hang the very heavy weight of our happiness on the very thin wire of our health. High-risk investment! People I know who have that wide, vertical, zipper-like scar down the middle of their chests are living proof that we all are only a pulse beat this side away from that side. Something as tiny as a blood clot, smaller, much smaller than a pea, if lodged in the wrong place, can suddenly turn our speech to a slur and reduce our steps to a shuffle . . . if that.

Two doors away from our home an entire family has been transformed from a life of activity, laughter, and hope to a quiet, introspective group of serious-looking, almost-out-of-touch people. Their only son—a brilliant, alive, bright collegian with a "sky's the limit" promising future—had a head-on collision with a semi.

Snap went the wire. Totaled car. Almost totaled driver. Toppled family. The boy, quasi-conscious, hardly resembles the young man who used to catch my passes on Thanksgiving afternoon and light fireworks with our Curt every Fourth of July. He may never walk again. Or talk. Or think clearly. Swiftly, silently, like a deep river, life moves right on as that family now turns in every night with a sigh. Health is a very tin wire, unable to support our happiness.

We hang the very heavy weight of our peace on the very thin wire of our possessions. We know better, but we still do it. Materialistic to the core, we convince ourselves that life *does* consist in the abundance of things we possess . . . that contentment is *not* limited to food and clothing . . . that the birds of the air and the lilies of the field don't know what they're missing without all those creature comforts.

Enter brushland fires on the furious wings of Santa Ana winds. Exit Southern California homes and appliances and furniture and beds to sleep in and cars to drive and peace. *Snap goes the wire* when the something as heavy as peace is so inseparably linked to something as thin as our possessions.

We're only asking for trouble when we lead ourselves to believe that our internal agitation will subside once we get that place in the mountains or a quaint condo at the beach or a little larger boat or a little better job or a microwave for Christmas or a second TV or stereo upstairs or an original oil in the living room or a Shop Smith in the garage or . . . or . . . It's not that owning any of that stuff is wrong—you know that—but when it's pursued in hopes of acquiring peace in the package, no way!

We also hang the very heavy weight of our security on the very thin wire of our savings. Solomon was right, as usual:

> Cast but a glance at riches, and they are gone,
> For they will surely sprout wings
> And fly off to the sky like an eagle (Proverbs 23:5, NIV).

That's part of the syndrome Haggai the prophet describes:

> You earn wages, only to put them in a purse with holes in it (Haggai 1:6).

Yussif, the Terrible Turk, needed that reminder two generations ago. He was a 350-pound wrestler who won it all in Europe before coming to America to grab more glory. Yussif challenged Strangler Lewis, our 200-pound champion grappler. The Turk tossed the Strangler around like a teddy bear and won. The new world champ picked up what he loved the most—money—5,000 dollars of it, which he demanded in U.S. gold. He crammed it into the money belt he wore around his huge circumference before setting sail back to Europe on the *S. S. Burgoyne*.

Many miles at sea, the ship began to sink. Yussif went over the side with his bulging belt full of gold still strapped around his enormous frame. The added weight was too much for even the Terrible Turk to stay afloat. Before the lifeboats could reach him, he plunged straight to the bottom of the Atlantic like an oversize iron cannon . . . never to be seen again. *Snap went the thin wire of the Turk's savings* . . . and all hope of his security. That true story illustrates these immortal words:

Riches profit not in the day of wrath . . . (Proverbs 11:4).

Whyte was right. The very thin wires of physical health, material possessions, and financial savings are no match for eternal heavyweights like lasting happiness, deep peace, and personal security.

Only one Person can step into a life
    and give it happiness even when health fails . . .
      and give it peace even when possessions fade . . .
        and give it security when savings fly away.

You can have it all—everything—on the wire called Jesus Christ. That wire will *never* snap. Not for a lifetime. Not for eternity.

Deepening Your Roots
Luke 16:1-15; 2 Corinthians 12:14; 1 Timothy 6:3-10; 1 Peter 5:1-9;
1 John 3:16-18

Branching Out
1. Look around your home and ask yourself, "Is there anything I can't live without?" If it possesses you, get rid of it!
2. Be generous. Test your back pocket. Be an anonymous giver today and send some money to a friend or enemy! Or, buy a sack of groceries for a family in need. But give it incognito.
3. Start a bank account and distribute all monies to those in need.

"Final Descent . . . Commence Prayer"

The following incident took place in 1968 on an airline bound for New York. It was a routine flight, and normally a boring affair. The kind of flights I like—uneventful. But this one proved to be otherwise.

Descending to the destination, the pilot realized the landing gear refused to engage. He worked the controls back and forth, trying again and again to make the gear lock down into place. No success. He then asked the control tower for instructions as he circled the landing field. Responding to the crisis, airport personnel sprayed the runway with foam as fire trucks and other emergency vehicles moved into position. Disaster was only minutes away.

The passengers, meanwhile, were told of each maneuver in that calm, cheery voice pilots manage to use at times like this. Flight attendants glided about the cabin with an air of cool reserve. Passengers were told to place their heads between their knees and grab their ankles just before impact. It was one of those I-can't-believe-this-is-happening-to-me experiences. There were tears, no doubt, and a few screams of despair. The landing was now seconds away.

Suddenly the pilot announced over the intercom:

We are beginning our final descent. At this moment, in accordance with International Aviation Codes established at Geneva, it is my obligation to inform you that if you believe in God you should commence prayer.

I'm happy to report that the belly landing occurred without a hitch. No one was injured and, aside from some rather extensive damage to the plane, the airline hardly remembered the incident. In fact, a relative of one of the passengers called the airline the very next day and asked about the prayer rule the pilot had quoted. No one volunteered any information on the subject. Back to that cool reserve, it was simply, "No comment."

Amazing. The only thing that brought out into the open a deep-down "secret rule" was crisis. Pushed to the brink, back to the wall, right up to the wire, all escape routes closed . . . only then does our society crack open a hint of recognition that God just might be there and—"if you believe . . . you should commence prayer."

Reminds me of a dialogue I watched on the tube the other night. The guy being interviewed had "come back alive" from Mount St. Helens with pictures *and sound track* of his own personal nightmare. A reporter for a local television station, he was in close proximity to the crater when the mountain suddenly rumbled to life, spewing steam and ash miles into the air. The reporter literally ran for his life. With camera rolling and the mike on. The pictures were, of course, blurred and murky, but his voice was something else. Periodically, he'd click on his gear.

He admitted after all this was played on the talk show that he only vaguely recalled saying many of those things. It was eerie, almost too personal to be disclosed. He breathed deeply, sobbed several times, panted, and spoke directly to God. No formality, no clichés—just the despairing cry of a creature in a crisis. Things like, "Oh, God, oh, my God . . . help! Help!! . . . Oh, Lord God, get me through. God, I need you, please help me; I don't know where I am"—more sobbing, more rapid breathing, spitting, gagging, coughing, panting—"It's so hot, so dark, help me, God! Please, please, please, please . . . oh, God!"

There's nothing to compare with crisis when it comes to finding out the otherwise hidden truth of the soul. Any soul. We may mask it, ignore it, pass it off with cool sophistication and intellectual denial . . . but take away the cushion of comfort, remove the shield of safety, interject the threat of death without the presence of people to take the panic out of the moment, and it's fairly certain most in the ranks of humanity "commence prayer."

David certainly did. When in "the slimy pit . . . the mud and the mire," he testifies that Jehovah heard his cry (Psalm 40:1-2). So did Paul and Silas in that ancient Philippian prison when all seemed hopeless (Acts 16:25-26). It was from "the deep" Jonah cried for help . . . choking on salt water and engulfed by the Mediterranean currents, the prodigal prophet called out in his distress (Jonah 2:1-4). Old King Nebuchadnezzar did, too, fresh off a siege of insanity when he had lost his reason and lived like a wild beast in the open field.

That former mental patient "raised his eyes toward heaven" and poured out the feelings of his soul to the Lord God, the very One the king had denied in earlier years (Daniel 4:29-37).

Crisis crushes. And in crushing, it often refines and purifies. You may be discouraged today because the crushing has not yet led to a surrender. I've stood beside too many of the dying, ministered to too many of the broken and bruised to believe that crushing is an end in itself. Unfortunately, however, it usually takes the brutal blows of affliction to soften and penetrate hard hearts. Even though such blows often seem unfair.

Remember Alexander Solzhenitsyn's admission:

> It was only when I lay there on rotting prison straw that I sensed within myself the first stirring of good. Gradually, it was disclosed to me that the line separating good and evil passes, not through states, nor between classes, nor between political parties either, but right through all human hearts. So, bless you, prison, for having been in my life.[7]

Those words provide a perfect illustration of the psalmist's instruction:

> Before I was afflicted I went astray,
> but now I obey your word.
>   It was good for me to be afflicted
> so that I might learn your decrees
>   (Psalm 119-67,71 NIV).

After crises crush sufficiently, God steps in to comfort and teach.

Feel headed for a crash? Engulfed in crisis? Tune in the calm voice of your Pilot.

He knows precisely what He is doing. And belly-landings don't frighten Him one bit.

Deepening Your Roots
Jonah 2:1-7; Luke 6:12; Philippians 4:6,7; 1 Peter 3:12

Branching Out
1. What's one lesson you've learned out of a crisis you've faced in the last six months?
2. Offer to pray for someone who is in the midst of a crisis. If possible, pray *with* the person. It will encourage him!
3. Try to comfort someone without giving advice. Just be there!

Restraint

Yesterday I got drunk.

Now wait a minute! Before you pick up your phone and notify six of your closest friends, let me explain. I was the victim of a dentist's drill. As he was about to do his thing on my ivories, he inserted eighty milligrams of *Nembutol* into my innocent bloodstream . . . resulting thereafter in a flow of words and actions that were *anything* but innocent, I am told. I have been informed that a tape recording was made which probably would call into question my ordination as well as cause my old Marine Corps drill instructor to blush. I am sure that the entire dental office—that motley group of rascals—has sufficient information to blackmail me. But they are sworn to secrecy. I hope.

My neighbors probably raised some eyebrows when my dear wife helped me out of the car and I staggered to the door, singing loudly. She informed me that I saw a mosquito and took a rather exaggerated swing at it. That led to a few other verbal expressions totally unlike a man of the cloth. When I awoke on the patio three hours later, my children were still giggling and snickering over my irresponsible homecoming. They also are sworn to secrecy. *They better be!*

Isn't it amazing what happens when the clamps of restraint are loosened? In some cases it's unbelievable! I would never, under normal conditions, declare: "Dentistry is a rip-off!" But I did yesterday. Right in front of my dentist and his drill team. I would not say to a young lady, "You talk too much—get out!" But that's exactly what I said to one of his capable assistants.

Thanks to *Nembutol,* I became an open book with no secret sections or hidden chapters containing guarded, private feelings and thoughts. For several unrestrained hours, my emotions ran rampant, and there's no way to recover the damage or remove the raw facts from that page of my life.

Of course, I was under the influence of a pain-killing drug, so I'm automatically excused, or so they assure me. Because of the circumstances, it's nothing more than a funny, harmless episode that makes us chuckle.

But that ain't always so.

The removal of restraint is usually excusable nor amusing. In fact, restraining ourselves is so important that God lists it as a fruit of the Spirit in Galatians 5:22-23. *Self-control,* another word for restraint, is honored by the Lord as the "anchor virtue" on His relay team that runs life's race for His glory. Many other voices are saying, "Let it all hang out" and "tell it like it is" and "hold nothing back" and "be open . . . express your feelings without restraint!" It's easy to buy that kind of advice. But when I go to my Bible, I find contrary counsel being marketed.

When we are angered, God instructs us to restrain ourselves. For proof, ponder Proverbs 14:29, 15:1, and

29:11, along with Ephesians 4:26-27. He further tells us not even to associate with one given to anger (Proverbs 22:24-25) or place him into leadership in the church (1 Timothy 3:2-3).

When we are tempted. He admonishes us to say no to lust and restrain our carnal nature (1 Corinthians 9:26-27; 2 Timothy 2:22).

When we are prompted to talk too much, He says, "Hold it! Better keep that to yourself!" (Proverbs 17:28; Job 13:5; Ephesians 4:29). Restraint of the tongue is a mark of wisdom. It is a slippery eel in need of being in check between our cheeks.

When food is stacked before us, God is pleased when we restrain ourselves from gluttony (Proverbs 23:1-2; 1 Corinthians 10:31-32). Being fat is often a telltale sign that control is lacking.

When money is to be earned, spent, saved, or invested, the use of restraint is the order of the day (Matthew 6:19-21; Luke 14:28-30; Romans 13:7-8).

Removing restraint from your life may seem like an exciting adventure, but it inevitably leads to tragedy. It's a lot like removing the brakes from your car. That may be daring and filled with thrills for awhile, but injury is certain. Take away the brakes and your life, like your car, is transformed into an unguided missile—destined for disaster.

Let's all learn a lesson from my extra-curricular escapades this week.

> When medicine is needed
> To dull the pain you're in,

Your actions may be silly
Yet they really are not "sin."

But when you willfully lose control
And set restraint aside,
Your actions then are sinful
And pain is multiplied.

Deepening Your Roots
Proverbs 17:14, 28; 22:24-25; 29:11; Ephesians 4:26-27; 2
   Timothy 2:22

Branching Out
1. Take one of these (food, tongue, money, or TV) and put
   a restraint on it by doing one of the following today: a)
   Eat *no* sweets; b) Don't say one critical remark; c) Don't
   spend any money in twenty-four hours; or d) Don't turn
   on the TV.
2. Play detective or researcher and find out what a "restraining order" means in our legal system.
3. You're bound to get angry this week. When you do, put
   a restraint on your tongue and mind; don't say a word
   and don't allow your mind to think critically of another.

Modeling God's Message

Hosea started a scandal in the parsonage. Why? Hold onto your hat—he married a prostitute. Talk about gossip! His name became a byword for "fool." Respect for him dropped to *zero*. His reputation was suddenly null and void. "Small wonder he is listed first among the *minor* prophets," some sneer . . . "He must have been some kind of a nut."

No. Wrong again, O critic. Hands down, Hosea was one of the most patient, tender, and loving of all the ancient prophets. Obedient to the core. Faithful to the end. "Then why in the world would a man such as he fall for a woman such as she?" Keep holding onto your hat—*God told him to!* That's right. God chose Hosea to model his message before all Israel, like a neon sign alongside the freeway. Like bold headlines in the Times. Of course, they didn't know it at first.

Barmaids giggled and merchants snickered as wedding bells rang across the valley. "Hey, did you hear the latest? Gomer got married—she got herself a preacher!" How humiliating it must have been. Everywhere they went on their honeymoon, she saw familiar faces. Insulting insinuations were uttered in smothered tones. Hosea must have bit his tongue until it bled. His marriage was an act of love . . . but to the public it was a joke. Before God, he stood justified and obedient. Before man, undiscerning and idiotic.

He must have replayed his memory hundreds of times, remembering God's directive:

> "Go, take to yourself a wife of harlotry and have children of harlotry . . ." (Hosea 1:2).

That's exactly what happened. She gave birth to a daughter and two sons while Hosea's wife—each was illegitimate—before she left home and went back into the streets. Hosea's wound was scarcely healed before he heard God's voice thundering from the heavens telling him to go out, find her, and bring her back into his home with the family. He did. For a couple of dollars and several bushels of barley *he bought her from others' arms* and claimed her as his own. Stretch your imagination and try to picture the love and dedication it took for Hosea to carry out God's instructions. The Living Bible paraphrases the statement:

> "Go and get your wife again and bring her back to you and love her, even though she loves adultery" (Hosea 3:1).

Not another soul in Israel heard the voice. Only Hosea. Therefore, rumors turned into ridicule as his fellow Jews watched with open mouths as he stopped down and lovingly carried her home. Little did the people realize they were observing a *living object lesson*—a divine pantomime—designed by God to illustrate the truth of their own lives.

From the fourth chapter to the end of his journal (once

Hosea had their attention), he exhorted them to listen . . . to hear . . . to return. Fifteen times he shouted, "RETURN!" but they never did. Even though he modeled the message as no other man on earth would be asked to do, they ignored the message as no other man on earth would be asked to do, they ignored his cries. He told them the truth: *"You* are the harlot! *You* have left Jehovah's love. *You* have resisted His affection and denied your marriage. He continues to call you His own . . . but *you* refuse to return. He loves you still. Return!'' They didn't. And three tragic years later Israel crumbled in the hands of Assyria.

Having a tough time modeling God's message? Feel unappreciated? Misunderstood? A little foolish? Ridiculed? So it goes, pilgrim. Rose gardens and pillow fights went out with the flood. These are rugged days. Without much padding in the seats or protection from the wind. It takes two things to keep from folding in the stretch: a tough hide and a tender heart. Hosea had both. And the scars to prove it. He died rejected and ignored.

So did Christ . . . until the resurrection.

Deepening Your Roots

Hosea 1:1-11; Hosea 3:1-5; Hosea 6:1; Acts 20:20-21; Luke
    15:8-10;
  Luke 11:32

Branching Out

1. Pray each day this week for someone you know who refuses to return to God.
2. Find a phrase or verse in the book that motivates you to remain faithful to God. Write the verse down and tape it to the inside of one of your kitchen cupboards that you open often, or the dashboard of your car.

Comparison

If I may select a well-known phrase from the cobwebs of the fourteenth century and wipe away the dust to garner your attention, it is:

COMPARISONS ARE ODIOUS

Odious . . . disgusting, detestable. If you want to be a miserable mortal, then compare. You compare when you place someone beside someone else for the purpose of emphasizing the differences or showing the likenesses. This applies to places and things as well as people. We can become so proficient at this activity that we sustain our addiction through an unconscious force of habit. Inadvertently, the wheels of our thinking slide over into the ruts of this odious mindset. Comparison appears in at least two patterns.

Pattern one: We compare ourselves with others. You can imagine the results already. Either you are prompted to feel smug and proud because your strengths outweigh his weaknesses . . . or, more often, you begin to feel threatened, inferior, and blue because you fail to measure up. Striving to emulate a self-imposed standard, you begin to slide from the pleasant plateau of the *real you* to the sinking sands of *I don't know who*. This sometimes leads to extreme role-playing where you try every way to adapt and alter your portrait to fit into someone else's frame. In simpler terms, you've pawned your real personality for a phony disguise. That's odious! Paul penned similar sentiments to a church that had become known for its comparison cliques:

We do not dare to classify to compare ourselves with those who commend themselves. When they measure themselves and compare themselves with themselves, they are not wise (2 Corinthians 10:12 NIV). *— there is no 2 Cor. 20.*

The very next verse tells us, "Our goal is to measure up to God's plan *for us*" (TLB). Not for someone else, but for you, personally. God's great desire for us is that we fulfill His plan for us in our *own* lives. In His way—His timing.

Pattern two: We compare others with others. This is worse than unfair, it's stupid. And often cruel. Children suffer most from well-meaning adults who catalog one child's talents in front of another child in some misbegotten effort at motivation. "Look at your sister Debbie. If she can get an A in math, so can you," Or, "See how easily Jimmy learned to swim? Why are you so afraid?" That sort of comparison is toxic—poisoning a child's self-image and smothering the very motivation the parent was seeking to kindle.

But children aren't the only victims. People compare preachers and teachers, church philosophies and orders of service, soloists and song leaders, personalities and prayers, wives and mothers, families and friends, homes and cars, salaries and jobs, scholarship and salesmanship, husbands and fathers, weights and worries, luxuries and limitations, pain and pleasure. That's odious! Why not accept people and places and things *exactly as they are?* Isn't that true maturity? Why not accept and adjust to differences as quickly and enthusiastically as God forgives our wrong and stands behind our efforts to try, try again? When love flows, acceptance grows.

Do you know what it is that kicks the slats out from under yesterday's routine and challenges us to rise and shine on today's menu of hours and minutes? It's *variety*. It's not the similarity of days that brings fresh motivation and stimulates enthusiasm—it's the lack of such, the varied *differences* that keep our attitudes positive and pleasing. To try to compare one day with another, then complain because today wasn't at all like yesterday, would be sheer folly and foolishness. The same principle applies to people.

Now listen very carefully: God, our wise and creative Maker, has been pleased to make everyone different and no one perfect. The sooner we appreciate and accept that fact, the deeper we will appreciate and accept one another, just as our Designer planned us. Actually, there is only one thing that would be worse than constant comparison, and that as if everyone were just alike.

Can you think of anything more odious?

Deepening Your Roots

2 Corinthians 10:1-18; Galatians 6:1-5; James 2:1-12
17-18

Branching Out

1. Identify a person you often compare yourself to. Is there a special way you try to act, or mimic, or dress like that person? If so, work on eliminating that action, etc. Return to the *real* you.
2. List three trademarks you like about yourself that others cannot copy (for example your smile).
3. Who are you trying to change? How about letting God have that responsible this week while you concentrate on accepting, encouraging, and loving that person?

Choosing Your Words

A good scriptural basis for the time I invest each week in my writing ministry would be Ecclesiastes 12:9-11. It says:

> In addition to being a wise man, the Preacher also taught the people knowledge; and he pondered, searched out and arranged many proverbs. The Preacher sought to find delightful words and to write words of truth correctly. The words of wise men are like goads, and masters of these collections are like well-driven nails. . . .

It is encouraging to see that Solomon didn't just dump a load of verbiage on the page. He "pondered," he "searched out," he "arranged" his thoughts in the teaching of knowledge. He also "sought to find delightful words" so as to write truth correctly, using *just* the right terms.

One of our church members recently said to me, "You know, I not only appreciate truth, I also appreciate the turn of a phrase." We all do! Our eyes get weary of grinding through the same old verbal ruts. They dance with delight upon some vivid vocabular excursion provided through the reading gate, along the picturesque path of well-chosen words. Shakespeare's coined phrase, "the mind's eye," tells us that he enjoyed walking the path as well as leading his readers down it.

But it was Bacon who said it best:

> Reading maketh a full man;
> Speaking, a ready man;
> Writing, an exact man.

When confused or uncertain, it often helps to do your thinking with pen and pad. Exercising the exacting discipline of squeezing thoughts through the fingertips (reducing elusive, shadowy ideas to "well-driven nails" on paper) is good for our minds. This enables us to become clear thinkers who communicate in concrete, well-arranged "goads" that puncture the thick clouds of sloppy thinking.

I chuckled as I read the following statements. They are literal sentences taken from actual letters received by public welfare departments. The use of wrong words or phrases illustrates the opposite of what I've been trying to say.

"I cannot get sick pay. I have six children. Can you tell me why?"

"I am glad to report that my husband who was reported missing is dead."

"I am very much annoyed to find that you have branded my boy illiterate, as this is a dirty lie. I was married a week before he was born."

"Mrs. Jones has not had any clothes for a year and has been visited by the clergy regularly."

J.B. Phillips, author of the modern English paraphrase

of the New Testatment, expresses in a nutshell all I am saying:

> . . . if . . . words are to enter men's hearts and bear fruit, they must be the right words shaped cunningly to pass men's defenses and explode silently and effectually within their minds.

To speak or write of Christ in a dull, boring manner is the greatest of all insults. Maybe this explains why so many missionary letters are quietly ignored and unread . . . or why so many attempts to share our faith are unsuccessful . . . or why so many discipline problems occur in Sunday school classes.

Let's get serious about removing the yawn on the other fella's face . . . especially you who are communicating about Jesus Christ. It's really true: A mist in the pulpit *does* create a fog in the pew.

Deepening Your Roots
Proverbs 22:17-21; 1 Corinthians 2:4,6-13; 2 Timothy 3:16-
    17;
    2 Timothy 4:1-5

Branching Out
1. Start reading a book that is more difficult than anything you've ever read.
2. Circle three words you don't know the meaning of. Look up their definitions.

Nit-Picking

Two congregations of differing denominations were located only a few blocks from each other in a small community. They thought it might be better if they would merge and become one united body, larger and more effective, rather than two struggling churches. Good idea . . . but both were too petty to pull it off. The problem? They couldn't agree on how they would recite the Lord's Prayer. One group wanted "forgive us our trespasses" while the other demanded "forgive us our debts." So the newspaper reported that one church went back to its trespasses while the other returned to its debts!

I read last week of two unmarried sisters who lived together. Because of a slight disagreement over an insignificant issue, they stopped speaking to each other. Unable and unwilling to move out of their small house, they continued to use the same rooms, eat at the same table (separately), and sleep in the same bedroom. Without one word. A chalk line divided the sleeping area into two halves, separating a doorway and fireplace. Each could come and go, cook and eat, sew and read without crossing over into her sister's domain. Through the night each could hear the breathing of the foe . . . but because neither was willing to take the first step to reconciliation and forgiveness, they coexisted *for years* in grinding silence.

Such silly skirmishes would be hilarious if they weren't so prevalent—and damaging. It's one thing to stand firm in major issues clearly set forth in Scriptures. It's another thing to pick fights over jots and titles. I never cease to be amazed at how petty we Christians can be over things that really don't amount to a hill of beans in the final analysis. But there we stand, ramrod rigid, nose to nose, as if heaven were holding its breath. Or to use Dean Rusk's phrase, "We negotiate eyeball to eyeball, and each side is afraid to blink."

> Believe as I believe—no more, no less;
> That I am right (and no one else) confess.
> Feel as I feel, think only as I think;
> Eat what I eat, and drink but what I drink.
> Look as I look, do always as I do;
> And then—and only then—I'll fellowship with you.

So wrote the captain of the nit-picking brigade.

While I was ministering at a Bible conference last summer I tightened my belt, rolled up my pants, and waded into this touchy subject. Afterwards I was concerned to hear from many in attendance that they had similar convictions but didn't feel free to say so since their pastors kept fanning personal flames and picking scabs off old sores. Preachers can be awfully small! Taking pot shots in sermons when we know nobody can answer back. Shooting jabs and pounding the pulpit on minor matters that make our adversary yawn and smile.

Instead of equipping and edifying the saints with solid, well-documented, carefully applied truth from the phasis that is divisive, argumentative, and blindly opinionated.

One lady at the conference informed me that she and her family had vacationed in Michigan and had seen the name of a church they would never forget:

The Original Church of God, Number Two.

Some things make the Lord smile. That kind of thing must make Him nauseated!

The greater lights of the Protestant Reformation were, of course, Tyndale, Luther, Calvin, Zwingli, Savonarola, Knox, and a half dozen other grand men of God. But one man who never got much press (but deserved much praise) was Philipp Melanchthon, a brilliant yet calm theologian who was Martin Luther's chief associate in leading the Reformation. In a day of major, far-reaching battles and fiery assaults from one man to another, this gentleman summed it up in a superb axiom:

> In essentials, unity; in nonessentials, liberty; in all things, charity.

In nonessentials, *liberty*. Remember that! Like cosmetics, guitars, kind of clothing, choice of car, expression of worship, entertainment preference, Sunday activities, style of music, philosophy of raising kids, cultural tastes, holiday traditions, luxury items, and scores of other such things. They supply fodder for nitpicking gossips. But in light of eternity—who cares? Not one is in the "essential" category.

How broad was Christ! On one occasion His twelve nailed a guy for casting out demons in the name of

Jesus . . . *"because he was not following us"* (Mark 9:38). The Lord braced them for doing that. He wanted them to get rid of any idea that they had a monopoly on miracles. He wouldn't tolerate their bigoted spirit. Our Savior *never* nit-picked.

As long as our knowledge is imperfect and our preferences vary and our opinions differ, let's leave a lot of room in areas that don't really matter. Diversity and variety provide the Body with a beautiful blend of balance . . . but a squint-eyed, severe spirit is a killer, strangling its victims with a noose of caustic criticism.

Just how much freedom do you really allow others to enjoy? Believe me, that's not a nit-picking question.

Deepening Your Roots
Mark 9:38-41; Acts 11:1-18; 1 Corinthians 9:1-18

Branching Out
1. Think of two actions a friend of yours does that "bothers" you decide whether or not these actions are "essentials" or "nonessentials." If they are nonessentials, then determine to allow the person the freedom to be himself.
2. Name three things or issues you are adamantly for or against. Now, do you give others the liberty to take an opposing view or do you insist they believe as you?

Staying Alert

Your mind is a muscle. It needs to be stretched to stay sharp. It needs to be prodded and pushed to perform. Let it get idle and lazy on you, and that muscle will become a pitiful mass of flab in an incredibly brief period of time.

How can you stretch your mind? What are some good mental exercises that will keep the cobwebs swept away? I offer three suggestions:

READ. You may be too crippled and too poor to travel—but between the covers of a book are ideas and insights that await the joy of discovery. William Tyndale was up in years when he was imprisoned. Shortly before his martyrdom he wrote to the governor asking for:

> . . . a warmer cap, a candle, a piece of cloth to patch my leggings. . . . But above all, I beseech and entreat your clemency to . . . permit me to have my Hebrew Bible, Hebrew Grammar, and Hebrew Dictionary, that I may spend time . . . in study.[8]

The powers of your perception will be magnified through reading. Read wisely. Read widely. Read slowly. Scan. Read history as well as current events . . . magazines and periodicals as well as classics and poetry . . . biographies and novels as well as the daily news and devotionals.

Don't have much time? Neither did John Wesley. But his passion for reading was so severe he made it a part of his schedule—he read mostly *on horseback*. He rode between fifty and ninety miles a day with a book propped up in his saddle . . . and got through *thousands* of volumes during his lifetime. Knowing that reading attacks thickness of thought, Wesley told many a younger minister either to read—or get out of the ministry.

TALK. Conversation adds the oil needed to keep our mental machinery running smoothly. The give-and-take involved in rap sessions, the question-answer dialogue connected to discussion, provides the grinding wheel needed to keep us keen.

Far too much of our talk is surface jargon . . . shallow, predictable, obvious, pointless. Talk is too valuable to waste. Leave the discussion of people and weather to the newscasters! Delve into issues, ideas, controversial subjects, things that really matter. Ask and answer "why" and "how" . . . rather than "what" and "when." Probe. Question. Socrates was considered wise—not because he knew all the answers, but because he knew how to ask the right questions. Few experiences are more stimulating than eyeball-to-eyeball, soul-to-soul talks that force us to *think* and *reason* through specifics. For the sheer excitement of learning, talk!

WRITE. Thoughts disentangle themselves over the lips . . . and through the fingertips. How true! The old gray matter increases its creases when you put it down on paper. Start a journal. A journal isn't a diary. It's more. A journal doesn't record what you do—it records what you *think*. It spells out your ideas, your feelings, your struggles, your discoveries, your dreams. In short, it helps you articulate *who you are*.

Who knows? Your memories might make the bestseller list in the year 2000. And speaking of that, why not try writing an article for your favorite magazine? Editors are on a constant safari for rare species like you.

Who knows? Your memoirs might make the bestseller list in the year 2000. And speaking of that, why not try writing an article for your favorite magazine? Editors are on a constant safari for rare species like you.

Deepening Your Roots
1 Kings 4:29-34; Proverbs 2:1-10; Proverbs 4:5-7; Isaiah 26:3;
Romans 8:5-11; romans 12:2

Branching Out
1. Read a book *this week!* Make it a fun challenge by setting up five goals while reading. Here are some ideas: a) read one chapter out loud to someone; b) read one chapter in the tub c) read one chapter in bed; d) read one chapter at lunch; c) read one chapter at a park.
2. Think of three questions from your reading. Now, go and find someone to talk to using these questions.

The Case Against Vanilla

I cannot imagine anything more boring and less desirable than being poured into the mold of predictability as I grow older. Few things interest me less than the routine, the norm, the expected, the status quo. Call it the rebel in me, but I simply cannot bear plain vanilla when life offers so many other colorful and stimulating flavors. A fresh run at life by an untried route will get my vote every time—in spite of the risk. Stay open-minded for a moment and I'll try to show you why.

John Gardner once pointed out that by their mid-thirties, most people have stopped acquiring new skills and new attitudes in any aspect of their lives. Does that jolt you? Stop and think, you who are over thirty. How long has it been since *you* acquired a new skill? How many brand-new attitudes have you adopted—personal, political, social, spiritual, financial—since you turned thirty?

Let's probe a little deeper. Do you drive to work the same way every morning? Are you compelled to approach a problem the identical way every time? Does a maverick (even *wild*) idea challenge you or cause you to retreat into the security of your shell? Have you lost that enthusiastic zest for discovery and adventure?

122

Say, you're older than you thought. You're older than you ought! God has arranged an "abundant life" for you, but it's slipping past. You're fast becoming addicted to the narcotic of predictability . . . and the longer you persist, the greater will be the pain of withdrawal.

Living and learning are linked; so are existing and expiring. Each day delivers a totally new set of circumstances and experiences. The same hours and minutes which capture the wonder of a child may deepen the rut of an adult.

Ever watched a preschooler's approach to life? His constant curiosity and probing inquisitiveness make every day completely fresh and exciting. To him, learning is natural; to the adult, it's a nuisance.

"Well," you rationalize. "I'm just too set. That's the way I am . . . you can't change me." *Who* can't change you? *God?* Like Israel of old, this sort of thinking puts limits on the Lord, discounting His power and denying His presence. Settling down to the hum-drum, bland diet of tasteless existence is a sure invitation for slackness and indolence to invade and plague your dwelling.

"So how do I break out?" you ask. "I guess I could row to Hawaii in a four-foot dinghy or schedule a February vacation in Iceland . . . maybe the family could tackle Everest this summer. . . ."

Unnecessary! Life abounds with everyday problems needing transformation into creative projects. Try taking life by the throat and achieve mastery over a few things that have haunted and harassed you long enough.

Or—how about a course at a nearby school this fall . . . or a serious study of some subject all on your own. Why not broaden yourself in some *new* way to the greater glory of God?

Remember our old friend, Caleb? He was eighty-five and still growing when he gripped an uncertain future and put the torch to the bridges behind him. At a time when the ease and comfort of retirement seemed predictable, he fearlessly faced the invincible giants of the mountain. Read Joshua 14 again. There was no dust on that fella. Every new sunrise introduced another reminder that his body and rocking chair weren't made for each other. While his peers were yawning, Caleb was yearning.

Every one of us was poured into a mold . . . but some are "moldier" than others. If you are determined and work quickly, you can keep the concrete of predictability from setting rock-hard up to your ears. Then again, if the risks and potential dangers of sailing your ship in the vast oceans of uncertainty make you seasick, you'd better anchor yourself near the shallow shore of security. Concrete sinks fast, you know.

Deepening Your Roots
Genesis 12:1-8; Joshua 14:1-15; Luke 6:17-28

Branching Out
1. It's time to acquire a new skill . . . so sign up today to take a class, or to play a new sport, or to finally learn how to drive, etc.
2. Break the routine. Go to a restaurant, or a grocery store, or library, etc., that you've never been to.
3. Buy a book on a topic you're interested in but have never pursued. Read it!

Rationalization

There I stood, the helpless victim of incredible pressure. The scene? (Immediately, you'll understand my plight.) A used car lot. A fast-talking salesman. Begging kids. The hour was late. You know, the whole bit. To top it all off, there sat the cutest little Volkswagen you can imagine. Bright red. And a *convertible!* What could I do but at least slip behind the wheel and see how it "fit." That did it. We *had* to take a drive, even if it was absolutely out of the question that we'd ever buy the thing. Top down, cool breeze blowing by, quiet engine. KBIG music flowing out of dual speakers, quick acceleration, only 4500 miles. Wow!

Suddenly, I cam back to reality. "This thing is a teen-ager's car," I could hear my conscience say. "How undignified can you get, Swindoll?" "Pretty undigni-fied," I snapped back. I mean, if one of my associate pastors can whip around town on his Honda 360 . . . why in the world should I drive a black, four-door Rambler sedan? And, furthermore, this thing's a collector's item—and my wife's crazy about it—and it gets great gas mileage—and it looks so lonely and unloved in the car lot—and I can always drive the station-wagon when I have a funeral—and—and—and.

Well, it's mine. Correction, it's *ours*. Rationalization and I bought it last month. And I'm still trying to believe it! Frankly, my biggest job is convincing folks that it's not my oldest son's car. I'm happy to lease it to him for a night or two (another rationalization); but make no mistake about it, Curt's dad owns it, not Curt!

All this has made me do a lot of thinking about our tendency to rationalize, which the dictionary defines as "providing plausible but untrue reasons for conduct." In other words, it's what we do when we substitute false explanations for true reasons . . . when we cloud our actual motives with a smoke screen of nice-sounding excuses. One of the reasons we do this is to dull the pain of reality. Another reason we do it is to quiet the sounds of guilt, that dragon whose deep bass voice is always ready to blast us with its deafening roar. Often we employ it to justify ourselves in the eyes of others.

Sometimes rationalization causes people to gloss over obvious sin. Aaron used it when his brother, Moses, faced him with his sin of fasioning a modern calf before the Israelites and encouraging them to worship it. Covered with gold dust, Aaron rationalized with wide eyes by saying, "You know the people yourself, that they are prone to evil. For they said to me, 'Make a god for us who will go before us. . . .' And I said to them, 'Whoever has any gold, let them tear it off.' So they gave it to me, and I threw it into the fire, and out came this calf" (Exodus 32:22-24).

Amazing! He was just an innocent bystander whose heart was as pure as the driven snow. After dumping in a few golden earrings and necklaces, out jumped this engraved calf! It was those wicked people . . . not him. Not on your life.

The Bible is replete with similar accounts. How much better it is to call a spade a spade. Instead of thinking of spiritual-sounding excuses or scriptural phrases the ease the conscience, let's come up front and just tell the truth . . . even though you can't make it sound "biblical." Along with being Christians, we are also quite human, remember.

If you own something really nice, don't try to hide it or diminish it because it has the appearance you fudged on your tithe. For goodness sake, enjoy it! You're unwise to *flaunt* it, but to attach some super-spiritual rationalization to it is totally unnecessary. And don't be afraid some missionary might find out. You'd be surprised how downright human and realistic most missionaries are!

So here's the principle: If you're wrong in what you're doing, stop. No rationalization will make it right. If you're right, relax. Ratinalization will only confuse the issue. The main thing is that you please the Lord with a clear conscience.

And that truth applies whether you drive a red VW convertible, a black Rambler, or a gold Continental (you lucky dog).

Deepening Your Roots
Genesis 20:1-6; Exodus 32:1-24; Acts 4:32-37; Acts 5:1-4;
    Acts 24: 10-16;
      Hebrews 13:15-18; 2 Timothy 1:3; 1 Peter 3:13-17

Branching Out
1. What did you rationalize in the last twenty-four hours?
   Admit it to someone else.
2. On your next big decision write down your proton reasons
   and then ask someone if they see any "rationalizing" in
   your thinking and choice.

Long Winds, Deep Roots

Mrs. Moses' cookbook surely had a special section on "A Thousand and One Ways to Fix Manna." Unless I miss my guess, she had tried them all . . . *ninety-nine times*. What potatoes are to Idaho, pineapples are to Hawaii, wheat to Kansas, and crab gumbo to New Orleans, manna was to the wandering Hebrews for forty weary years (Exodus 16:35). They boiled it, baked it, broiled it, barbequed it, breaded it, and buttered it. They ate it cold, hot, raw, cooked, sliced for sandwiches, baked pies, and sprinkled on their cereal. You name it—they tried it.

When everyone came in to eat, they didn't ask, *"What's for supper?"* but, *"How'd you fix it?"* Mealtime was about as exciting as watching paint dry or listening to the minutes of last year's meeting. The most familiar sound around the table was not slurping or smacking. It was *gagging*. Oh, how they hated it. Numbers 11 tells us they actually lost their appetite because they were sick of all that manna. Everyone remembered the fish, cucumbers, leeks, onions, garlic, and melons back in Egypt—and you've got to be pretty miserable to dream of a combination plate like that.

Hold on here! Let's fine-tune that picture. A closer

130

look at the circumstances paints a different scene altogether. Let me explain. These people didn't have to work for their food or clothing . . . not one day for forty years! Every morning, instead of going out to get the newspaper like you and I do, they gathered up the day's groceries—delivered to their front door. For forty years! There was no inflation, no sales tax, and no long lines at the checkout counter. Just a constant, daily supply of nourishing food. As a matter of fact, God called it *food from heaven . . . the bread of angels* (Psalm 78: 24-25).

Accompanying this morning miracle was the faithful cloud by day and the comforting fire by night which gave them visible assurance of God's presence and protection. When thirst came, He quenched it with water that flowed from rocks like rivers. Those people enjoyed a perpetual catering service without cost, limit, labor, or hassle. All they had to do was show up, look up, eat up, and clean up. Yet for all of this, they came to the place where they resented heavenly-cooked angels' bread. Already having much, they now wanted more. Having plenty, they now wanted variety. Having tired of manna, they now wanted meat.

Exodus 16:4 provides additional insight often overlooked:

> . . . the LORD said to Moses, "Behold, I will rain bread from heaven . . . and the people shall go out and gather a day's portion every day, that I may test them. . . ."

Look carefully at the last five words. The manna was more than it appeared to be—basically, it was a *test*.

It was God's examination, carefully planned, wisely implemented, and administered on a daily basis (note in the verse especially the phrase *every day*). God custom-designed the diet to be a day-after-day, week-after-week test of their obedience, their patience, and their determination to persevere in spite of the monotony of the manna. The team results came back with a big red ''F'' across the front.

When I was only a boy, the Swindolls occasionally enjoyed a family reunion at my grandfather's bay cottage near the Gulf in deep South Texas. Since the crowds were so large, we'd hire the same man each time to help with the cooking. His name was *Coats*. His skin was as black as a cast-iron skillet and his quick smile and quaint comments are a lasting memory to me. I remember standing near Coats one evening at sunset, watching him smear the sauce on the chunks of beef cooking slowly over a pit of coals. He was telling me about his life, which had been etched with trouble and tragedy. He rubbed his big, leathery hand through my white hair as he knelt down to my height and said:

> Little Charles—the hardest thing about life
> is that it's so daily.

A simple way to say it, but what could be more true? *Life is so daily*. The tests that come like a flash and last no longer than a dash seldom do more than bring a brief crash. But the marathons—the relentless, incessant, persistent, continual tests that won't go away—ah, these are the ones that bruise but build character. Since virtue is not hereditary, God dispenses His tests of manna to each saint in each generation, watching to see if there will be a heavenly appetite to accept a heavenly food.

If finding God's way in the suddenness of storms makes our faith grow broad, then trusting God's wisdom in the "dailyness" of living makes it grow deep. And strong.

Whatever may be your circumstances—however long it may have lasted—wherever you may be today, I bring this remember: The stronger the winds, the deeper the roots, and the longer the winds . . . the more beautiful the tree.

Deepening Your Roots
Exodus 16:1-36; Isiah 40:21-31; Matthew 13:1-29; Ephesians 3:14-21

Branching Out
1. Try eating tuna, eggs, cottage cheese, or chicken for three meals in a row to sense how the Israelites felt eating manna over and over.
2. Supply food for someone this week either by delivering a meal, sack of groceries, or treating him to dinner. Tell the person about this assignment and something you learned from today's "Deepening Your Roots" study.
3. Instead of griping or complaining about that boring job or a chore (e.g., picking up after your kids for the nth time, or taking out the trash again), do it with a thankful heart. Be glad you have that job, those kids, strength, etc.

Taking Time

Eight words are brashly smeared across the dashboard of the speedboat tied up at Gulf Shores, Alabama. They reflect the flash and flair of its owner whose fast life is often publicized in sporting news across America. In the off-season, the left-handed speedster in the Gulf of Mexico resembles a shiftless, beachcombing drifter with his stubble beard, disheveled hair, and darting eyes rather than one of the highest-paid quarterbacks in Oakland Raider history. If his profession doesn't fit his looks, his nickname certainly does. *SNAKE*. As swift and sneaky in a swamp as he is on the field, Ken Stabler knows one speed . . . full throttle.

So we shouldn't be surprised to read the saucy sign on his dashboard that warns all passengers:

GET IN, SIT DOWN, SHUT UP, HANG ON

If you plan to ride with Snake Stabler, be ready for one sustained roar during the trip. Somehow there's this itch inside him that isn't scratched, apart from that scream of an engine and the blur of salt water waves rushing beneath to the tune of 80 + miles per hour. Once you get in and sit down, you have the distinct feeling that shutting up and hanging on come naturally. Once you've committed yourself to such an accelerated velocity, nothing short of survival really matters.

All that's OK if survival is the only thing that matters. If, however, the things that make life rich and meaningful to us (and those traveling with us) involve more than survival, then speed is an awfully thin wire to hang genuinely desire some depth to emerge, some impact to be made, some profound and enduring investment to cast a comforting shadow across another's life (your child, a friend, whomever), it is essential that we slow down . . . at times, stop completely. And think. Now . . . not later. Don't you dare put this off another day!

My oldest son and I were lingering in a local gift shop time ago. Our eyes fell upon a row of large posters that were framed and stacked together. We laughed at some nutty ones, we studied some serious ones . . . but one stood alone as our favorite. When Curt found it, he said nothing at first, then moments later he whispered quietly, "Wow, Dad, that's good!" It was a picture of a misty morning on a calm lake. In a little skiff were a father and his son looking at the two corks floating at the ends of their fishing lines. The sun was tipping its hat over the mountains in the distance. Stretching across the scene was peace, refreshment, easygoing small talk. Two wistful words beneath the border appropriately released the message:

TAKE TIME

In my younger years I was irritated with the well-worn tune attached to the old-fashioned sounding words of William Longstaff:

Take time to be holy,
Speak oft with thy Lord;

Take time to be holy,
The world rushes on. . . .

Twenty-five years, four children, many miles and mistakes later, those words make a lot of sense. They are like the psalmist's plea in Psalm 46:10.

CEASE STRIVING AND KNOW THAT I AM GOD. . . .

Or our Lord's counsel in Matthew 11:280

COME TO ME . . . I WILL GIVE YOU REST.

Eight calm words from David. Eight restful words from Jesus, who never *rushed* anywhere! How unlike those eight panic words from the speedboat!

Deepening Your Roots
John 2:1-12; John 7:1-9; John 10:40-11:23

Branching Out
1. Don't rush through any task today. Take your time.
2. Force yourself to not use the car today. Instead, walk to work (if possible), or to school, or to the store.
3. Rather than rush through dinner tonight, make everyone stay at the table an extra fifteen minutes. Relax together and talk about something you're looking forward to seeing or doing.

Of Roots and Wings

"Grab here, *amigo*," I grabbed.

"Hold tight, *por favor*," I held on.

"When you come back toward shore and I blow whistle, you pull cord *pronto!*"

Within seconds I was airborne. A loud "whoosh," a long, strong jerk, and I was 300 feet or so above the picturesque beach at Puerto Vallarta. You guessed it . . . my first try at parasailing. Four-and-a-half minutes of indescribable ecstasy sandwiched between a few seconds of sheer panic. Talk about fun!

Above me was the bluest, clearest sky you could imagine. Behind me was a full-blown, dazzling red and white parachute. Down in front, attached to my harness and a long yellow rope, was a speed boat at full throttle. Below, the turquoise sea, various sailing vessels, a long row of hotels, sun bathers the size of ants, and one beautiful lady wondering if she would soon be a widow.

The wind whipped through my hair and tore at my swimsuit. But the sensation of flying in silence with nothing surrounding me besides a few nylon straps was absolutely breathtaking. The spectacular view plus the enjoyable feelings of soaring like a seagull introduced me to an adventurous freedom rarely encountered by earth dwellers.

I must confess, for those few minutes I lost all concern for things that otherwise occupy my attention. Self-consciousness vanished. Worries fled away. Demands and deadlines were forgotten, strangely erased by the swishing sound of the wind. *It was glorious!* I don't believe that as an adult I've ever felt quite so free, so unencumbered, so completely removed from others' expectations and my own responsibilities.

Such are the benefits of leisure. True, authentic, carefree relaxation. The kind Jesus had in mind when He encouraged His twelve to come apart and rest awhile. How easy to forget the necessity of recreation . . . how quick we are to discount its value! In our neurotic drive for more, more, more, we ignore how uncreative and boring we become. All roots and no wings has the makings of Dullsville, U.S.A. Life closes in and takes the shape of a chore instead of a challenge. Fun and laughter, originally designed by God to remove the friction of monotony from the machinery of existence, begin to be viewed as enemies instead of friends. Intensity, that ugly yet persuasive twin of hurry, convinces us we haven't the right to relax . . . we must not take time for leisure . . . we can't afford such rootless, risky luxury. Its message is loud, logical, sensible, strong, *and wrong*.

We *do* need relief. We *must* discover ways to loosen the strings periodically and fly. To quote the venerable prophet, Vance Havner, "If we don't come apart, we *will* come apart."

Find what brings you relief and take time to soar!

A motorcycle ride along quiet trails.

An afternoon of sailing.

A mountain to climb.

A weekend on the slopes.

A journey of some significant distance on a bike.

A long run on a longer beach.

A leisurely river ride in a rubber raft.

Isn't it time to think seriously about that trip you've talked about for so long? Or that fishing expedition? Or that weekend camp-out with your good friends? Try some winged adventure that turns you on and expands your world and frees your mind and calms your nerves. Don't wait! Quit worrying about the risk or complaining about the cost. We keep coming back to those two essentials—roots and wings—but it's my observation that most of us are long on the former and short on the latter.

Take it from a rooke parasailer . . . go for it! Stop thinking *"mañana."* Grab here. Hold on tight, *amigo.*

Deepening Your Roots
Proverbs 11:24; Acts 3:17-19; 1 Corinthians 16:17, 18; Philemon 7:20-21

Branching Out
1. Take time out sometime today and do one of the following: go watch some airplanes take off or land; eat lunch alone outside and in a new location; go fly a kite; go fishing; go sailing; or take a nap in the park.
2. Have you ever been camping with your family? Plan a trip this month. If you don't have the equipment, borrow it. Enjoy flexing your wings a little, my friend.

Operation Relaxation

Some days start right, others end right. This one did both, for a change. During the daylight hours things fell into place and as the evening approached, it got better! As planned, I got home before Monday Night Football. The smell of homemade clam chowder was lingering inside the front door. After hugging the kids and kissing the cook, I settled into my favorite chair . . . loosened my tie, and kicked off my shoes. Detecting a new aroma, our miniature schnauzer, Heidi, moved across the room.

Upstairs, our two youngest were fiddling around with a rabbit, two hamsters, and a guinea pig—the protesting squeals of man and beast wafting down the stairwell. Our older daughter (finally off the phone) was out front enjoying the companionship of a neighbor gal . . . and a couple of guys, if I'm not mistaken. Curt was on the floor in his room strumming out a few chords on his steel strings—singing "Raindrops Keep Fallin' on My Head" as a lazy California sun was saying goodbye for the day. In between chopped onions and diced potatoes, Cynthia had doubled over with laughter as she tried to finish a chapter of Erma Bombeck's, *The Grass Is Always Greener Over the Septic Tank*.

No amount of money could buy the feeling that swept

over me—incredible contentment . . . an inner sense of fulfillment . . . a surge of release and relief as the noise and pace of the world were strangely muffled by the sounds and smells of home. The comfortable fingers of nostalgia wrapped themselves around me and warmed me within.

Although my "to-do" list was mostly "yet to be done," the day was over. Tomorrow would usher in its own sets of needs and responsibilities, but that was tomorrow. We all enjoyed supper (at half time, of course), then knocked out the cleanup in exactly five minutes . . . a new Swindoll world knocked out the cleanup in exactly five minutes . . . a new Swindoll world record . . . as we moved faster than six speeding bullets, laughing like mad.

What therapy! How essential! And yet, how seldom families really relax. It's almost as though we're afraid to shift into neutral and let the motor idle. With a drive that borders near the neurotic, we Americans hit the floor running at 6: 00 A.M., then drop, exhausted, at 12:00 midnight . . . scarcely able to remember what transpired during that eighteen-hour episode of relentless actions and words. If God is going to get our attention, He'd better plan on (1) making an appointment, (2) taking a number, or (3) pulling us over with a flashing blue light on the freeway—otherwise, forget it! Strange, isn't it, that we place such a high priority on achivement we actually feel guilty when we accomplish nothing over a period of several hours. Such an experience requires justification when others ask, "What did you do last night?"

I visited a small town during a recent trip through central Oregon. It was one of those places that was so relaxed I found myself getting antsy. Life moves along there about the speed of a glacier. You know . . . the type of town where people gather to watch hub caps rust. I asked my friend:

"How do you stand it? Doesn't the slow pace drive you crazy?"

He responded with a smile, "Well, it took us about eight months to unwind. You gotta *learn* how to relax, Chuck. It isn't something that you do automatically. Now, we love it."

I've thought a lot about that. Relaxing isn't automatic. It's a skill that must be learned . . . cultivated. And since most of us don't live in a sleepy little town, here are a few suggestions to help you develop a workable plan.

1. Block out several evenings each month on your calendar. Make special plans to do *nothing*—except something you (or your family) would enjoy.

2. Loosen up the tight wires of your life by not taking yourself so seriously . . . nor your job. Sure, some things *are* terribly serious—but not everything. The old Greek motto is still true: "You will break the bow if you keep it always bent."

3. Look for times during each day when something humorous or unusual makes laughter appropriate . . . then laugh out loud! That helps flush out the nervous system. Solomon tells us this is good medicine.

4. When you relax, *really relax* . . . blow it . . . enjoy the leisure . . . let out all the stops . . . ignore what

some narrow-minded, squint-eyed critic might think or say. For sure, you'll get flak from those who burn out.

I'm of the opinion that a relaxed, easygoing Christian is miles more attractive and effective than the rigid, uptight brother who squeaks when he walks and whines when he talks.

Deepening Your Roots
2 Samuel 16-13-14; Psalm 23: 1-3

Branching Out
1. Do one of the suggestions above.
2. Have everyone in the family secretly write down a thing to do (that doesn't cost anything). Put all the ideas in a box or hat and one of you draw one card. You must do whatever the person requests.

Growing Strong

I hate to break the news, but those hazy, lazy days of summer are coming to an end. At least for *Growing Strong in the Seasons of Life*. It's been a relaxing three months! How about you? Did you ease up, include a few more refreshment breaks, and stay cooler this year? Hope so. Now it's time to usher in autumn, that colorful season that brings with it a flood of memories. Speaking of memories, what's your favorite one this summer?

Conclusion

Some verses from the Bible make us smile. We have enjoyed them together as we considered a few such verses through the pages of this book. some references are penetrating and convicting as they cause us to look into the mirror of truth and face facts. We've considered a number of those, too. Others are comforting, giving us hope to go on, regardless. A few introduce us to brand new scenes we'd never seen before. Maybe that has happened as you've worked your way through the pages.

There is one verse, however,that never fails to take us by the shoulders and shake us awake. It comes to my mind because it draws upon a word picture of seasons to make its point. You may recall reading it before:

"Harvest is past, summer is ended,
And we are not saved" (Jeremiah 8:20).

Does that describe *you?* If so, may I suggest that you come to terms with this need. Seasons follow a cycle: winter, spring, summer, autumn . . . so that the earth might enjoy all the things its Creator designed for it to enjoy.

Your life is, in many ways, the same. Multiple seasons, not a long, monotonous marathon of pointless futility; but variety, peaks and valleys, change and color. How tragic to move through the seasons without realizing their ultimate purpose! And what is that?

Go back to the verse. Read it aloud. The purpose is obvious: that we might *be saved* . . . that we might not trust in ourselves but in Jesus Christ, our Creator Lord . . . and, in doing so, receive from Him the assurance of abundant life now and eternal life forever.

Throughout this book I've been truthful with you. Now it's your turn to be truthful with yourself. Are you absolutely certain that you possess His gifts of forgiveness and purpose? You can have that assurance if your traveling Companion through the year is the Son of God. He alone can give meaning to the cycle as He enables you to grow strong in all the seasons of your life.

FOOTNOTES

1. Bruce Larsen, *The One and Only You* (Waco, Texas: Word Books, 1974), pp. 84-85. Adaptation by permission of Word Books, Publisher, Waco, Texas 76703.
2. Leslie B. Flynn, *Great Church Fights* (Wheaton: Victor Books, 1976), p. 105.
3. Flynn, p. 104.
4. Bruce Larsen and Keith Miller, *The Edge of Adventure* (Waco, Texas: Word Books, 1974), p. 156.
5. Dorothy Hsu, *Mending* (Ft. Washington, Pa.: Christian Literature Crusade). Used by permission.
6. F. B. Meyer, *Christianity in Isaiah* (Grand Rapids: Zondervan Publishing House, 1950), p. 9.
7. Alexander Solzhenitsyn, *The Gulag Archipelago,* quoted in Philip Yancey, *Where Is God When It Hurts?* (Grand Rapids: Zondervan Publishing House, 1977), p. 51.
8. J. Oswald Sanders, *Spiritual Leadership* (Chicago: Moody Press, 1967), p. 94.

One More Day
Daily Meditations for the Chronically Ill
Sefra Kobrin Pitzele

Each Day a New Beginning
Daily Meditations for Women
Hazelden Foundation

Twenty-Four Hours a Day
Hazelden Foundation

Codependent No More
*How to Stop Controlling Others
and Start Caring for Yourself*
Melody Beattie